THE PILGRIMS' WAY

Shrines and Saints in Britain and Ireland

John Adair   Photographs by Peter Chèze-Brown

with 199 illustrations, 20 in colour, and 2 maps

Thames and Hudson

Filmset and printed in Great Britain by BAS Printers Limited, Over Wallop, Hampshire
Bound in Great Britain

Half-title page *Wrought-iron screen dividing the south transept from the choir aisle in Winchester Cathedral, twelfth or thirteenth century.*

Title page *The 'Pilgrims' Way' to Canterbury on Reigate Hill, Surrey.*

Right *St Josse of Brittany as a pilgrim, with staff, heavy shoes, knapsack, and book. (Sixteenth-century figurine in the Hofkirche at Innsbruck, Austria)*

Contents

Preface

This book is written primarily to serve as a companion to those who wish to follow in the footsteps of pilgrims who travelled the roads of Britain and Ireland during the Middle Ages. But it is more than a guide to the shrines that have survived from medieval times. For the following pages are an opportunity for you the reader to join at least some of those pilgrims in your imagination. Although I may lack the hearty *bonhomie* of Harry Bailey, the shrewd host of the Tabard Inn at Southwark, who so ably conducted Chaucer's pilgrims to Canterbury, yet I hope to lead you as safely – and perhaps as merrily – upon this longer pilgrimage. If we are to approach the heart of pilgrimage, let us borrow the clothes of medieval men and women, feel the hardness of the roads under their bare penitential feet, and above all see the shrines in those cool dim cathedrals through their thankful eyes.

Our mental journey can only begin after some spadework has removed the earth of secular centuries which covers the pilgrim's way. Therefore I make no apology for an introduction explaining how the practice of pilgrimage arose, developed and declined in Europe during the Middle Ages. For British pilgrimages need to be set in the framework of the Christian religion of that time, and to be seen in the context of a universal practice embracing the whole of Europe and the Holy Land. As we travel, I shall include many short accounts of saints' lives and miracles and some digressions into history, so that we may share something of the pilgrims' beliefs and their hopes as they approached their chosen shrines. The primary sources which bring the story to life range from the richly imaginative medieval lives of the saints, many of them based on first-hand knowledge or reliable early tradition, to the objective descriptions and urbane comments of the great Dutch humanist Erasmus, who visited two English shrines at the beginning of the sixteenth century.

We shall take to the road and first explore the pilgrim ways to the shrine of St Thomas Becket at Canterbury. From there, the centre of both Christianity and pilgrimage in Britain during the Middle Ages, we can wander at leisure from shrine to shrine, like a band of palmers, until we have seen and walked in all the holy places: from London to the West Country, in East Anglia and along the Roman roads through the Midlands, to Durham and beyond the hills of Wales, and finally to Scotland and across the sea to Ireland.

Then comes the reckoning. For if we are to be more than tourists our concern will embrace not only outward forms but also inward meanings.

In the last chapter we shall therefore have to return to our starting point in the secular present and ask ourselves – as the medieval pilgrims did when they came home – what the pilgrimage has done for us. Perhaps our answers may be different from those of our medieval forefathers, but no less profound.

John Lydgate presenting his poem 'The Pilgrim' to Thomas Montacute, Earl of Salisbury. Lydgate (who was born about 1370) is dressed as a pilgrim, with hat, scrip and staff. (British Library, London, Harley MS 4826)

To be a pilgrim

The pilgrim instinct must be deep in the human heart, although it finds different expressions according to time, place and culture. Obviously it is not peculiar to Christianity: the Hindu, Buddhist and Muslim religions all value these journeys to a saint's shrine or some other sacred place. Pilgrimages appear in ancient Semitic and Egyptian religions in the centuries before Christ and they still occur today, both within and beyond the limits of Christianity – sometimes in purely secular forms. Yet there were elements, like so many magnets, in the early Christian faith which located, drew out and defined the pilgrim instinct in medieval men and women. It led to the development of pilgrimage as a social practice no less creative and interesting in all its ramifications than a great cathedral.

Pilgrimages in Christian history probably pre-date the first literary mentions of them. In 156 the author of *The Martyrdom of Polycarp* (Bishop of Smyrna in the Roman province of Asia), can speak of that bishop's bones as 'more valuable than refined gold'. But relics – in a strict sense the mortal remains of a saint – had already acquired a broader meaning which covered all objects which had been in touch with the saint's remains or even his tomb. In Chapter 19 of Acts it is asserted that God worked singular miracles through Paul: 'when handkerchiefs and scarves which had been in contact with his skin were carried to the sick, they were rid of their diseases and the evil spirits came out of them.' Christians continued to believe that God could work miracles of healing through saints' bones or *brandea* (cloths which had been in touch with them), as surely as he had used their earthly lives. Above all their tombs provided a location for the healing, forgiving and guiding powers of God.

Naturally the early Christians turned their faces and steps towards Palestine, which they conceived to be one vast relic. For the physical contact with Jesus Christ had hallowed Palestine for all time, transforming it into the *Holy Land* of Christian imagination. Some parts of it may have seemed more holy than others. As Jesus had immersed himself in the Jordan so all pilgrims made their way thither and did the same, believing the waters to be a most powerful relic because the same river in which they bathed had once touched the sacred body of the Saviour. On their way home through Jericho they plucked palm leaves and stuck them in their broad hats, hence their popular name of 'palmers'.

The thin trickle of pilgrims to Palestine in the third century grew into a stream in the fourth century. Novelties thrown like dry sticks upon the steadily burning fire of their devotion caused sudden bursts of enthusiasm. A distinguished pilgrim, the Emperor Constantine's mother Helena, was shown in a dream the whereabouts of the True Cross in Jerusalem (a cave under the Holy Sepulchre Church), and other 'inventions' or discoveries were soon recorded. Two monks, for example, claimed to have found the head of John the Baptist among the ruins of Herod's palace. Before long, many of the relics of the principal actors and other material props of the Biblical drama were on display in some church or other in the Holy Land. (When I lived on the Mount of Olives some years ago I had pointed out to me the footprint of Jesus in the rock left at his Ascension, and doubtless medieval pilgrims saw the same sight. In the dark labyrinthine corners of the Church of the Holy Sepulchre itself there were still to be seen showcases full of relics – brown bones, rusty iron and faded cloth – which survived from those days, with the elegant Latin crosses of the pilgrims incised into the walls all around them.) The traffic of pilgrims to the Holy Land soon attracted commercial interest. The travel memoirs of a Spanish nun called Etheria, written about 400, mention well-established lodgings and guides willing for a fee to lead pilgrims around the sacred sites.

By this time, however, Europe had acquired its own centres of pilgrimage. Besides the bones of the chief apostles, Peter and Paul, the imperial capital of Rome possessed the relics of the martyrs killed during the persecutions which came to their bloody climax under Diocletian. By the very fact of martyrdom these men and women acquired instant sanctity: indeed, when St Vincent was executed by Roman soldiers the Christian bystanders rushed forward to dip their clothes in his blood. In the mid-fourth century a Roman liturgical calendar could list about thirty sanctuaries of saints in or around the city. Four Anglo-Saxon kings journeyed to worship in Rome. One of them, the celebrated King Ine of Wessex, having defeated all his enemies, even resolved to renounce his kingdom in order to live out his days in the city of the apostles.

Meanwhile, shrines of lesser saints and martyrs had appeared, like mushrooms after rain, all over Europe. Every church coveted a holy relic. In the sixth century Pope Gregory the Great sent to St Augustine and his fellow missionaries in England 'all things necessary for the worship of the church, namely sacred vessels, altar linen, ornaments, priestly vestments, and relics of the holy apostles and martyrs'. The second Council of Nicaea (787) gave recognition to a growing custom by decreeing that no church should be consecrated without relics. They were placed in the altar or upon it in a reliquary, or in a crypt beneath it, like the bones of Peter and Paul at Rome. The words of the Book of Revelation may be the earliest reference to this practice: 'I saw under the altar the souls of them that were slain for the word of God, and for the testimony which they held.' A good English example of such a crypt is that which once housed the relics of St Cedd at Lastingham in Yorkshire. We shall come across others at Ripon and Hexham (pp. 150–51).

Although the countries of Europe could call upon the posthumous services of their own early martyrs to provide relics for consecrating churches, these were too few in number to meet the need. Consequently they were augmented by an untidy and largely spontaneous mixture of

The crypt of Lastingham Church, associated with St Cedd (brother of St Chad), who founded the monastery and died there in 664. Most of the massive structure is Norman, but the fat bases of the pillars probably come from the earlier Saxon church.

relics imported from Rome and the Holy Land, of others 'invented' or transported by miraculous means, and of the bones of later indigenous martyrs and saints. Thus supply kept pace with the growing demand. The development of large public and private collections of relics, such as the one accumulated by the emperors in Byzantium, further stimulated the market. For market it had become: as early as 400 St Augustine of Hippo complained of 'the hawking about of the limbs of martyrs'. The unsavoury trade flourished for centuries, the precursor to our modern traffic in antiques and antiquities. To explain the resultant flood of holy articles it was widely believed that all relics possessed the miraculous power of self-multiplication, not unlike the mystery of the Eucharist.

In the early Middle Ages each country possessed some shrines to its native saints. Bede, who died in 735, mentions visits from the fifth century onwards to the graves of such saints as Alban, Oswald, Chad and Cuthbert. The saints of the succeeding ages were not always martyrs. Confessors – those who had witnessed to the faith by sufferings short of death or by the self-imposed cross of a holy and blameless life – were also sometimes accorded the status of saints. The test usually lay in the efficacy of their relics to work miracles. If miracles occurred which could be directly associated with a dead person or his relics, then he was acclaimed a saint by his neighbours, and sometimes his fame would spread throughout the region. In Norfolk alone during the Middle Ages there were some seventy places associated with such saints or their relics visited by pilgrims. In later times such local, popular and fairly instant recognition gave way to the long, formal and distant process of canonization in Rome, with a corresponding decrease in the number of saints.

Medieval pilgrims' badges of lead, found in London and now in the Museum of London. The first three relate to the Canterbury pilgrimage – two representations of St Thomas Becket's mitred head, referring to the Corona *shrine (see p. 68), and an initial T for Thomas framing the scene of Henry II doing penance before the Saint (see pp. 37–38). The fourth, a crown, indicates a royal saint, probably St Edward the Confessor (see pp. 74–77), and dates from the fourteenth century.*

Whatever their type or origin, only a few of the shrines of Europe acquired what could be called international popularity. After Rome came undoubtedly Santiago de Compostela in northern Spain, where in 816 the body of St James was said to have been wonderfully rescued from the Atlantic breakers. France contained such shrines as the tomb of St Martin at Tours, and the reputed head of John the Baptist at Amiens. Besides owning the authentic remains of St Boniface, Germany took pride in the Holy Coat at Trier, which all Europe believed to be the seamless robe of the Crucifixion story, and the magnificently jewelled relics of the Magi, known as the Three Kings of Cologne. In Italy they venerated the Holy House of Loreto, the reputed home of Jesus in Nazareth which was miraculously transported to this location in 1295. The tomb of St Francis and his church of Portiuncula near Assisi, together with the shrine of St Anthony at Padua, were already well-established. Of the English shrines only those of Our Lady of Walsingham (see pp. 114–20) and St Thomas Becket at Canterbury (pp. 35–73) belonged to the first rank of popularity in Europe as a whole.

The great growth in the number of pilgrimages in the Middle Ages owes much to their prescription as penances. After a Christian had made his confession the priest gave him absolution, thereby freeing him from guilt but not from the punitive consequences of his sins in purgatory or hell. A penance such as a pilgrimage made with bare feet served in place of all or part of that punishment. Those convicted by the courts of serious crimes often undertook their pilgrimage clothed in sackcloth and ashes, their limbs bound with iron fetters.

Indulgences were essentially written certificates to the effect that a period in purgatory had been remitted. In preaching the first crusade at Clermont in 1095 Pope Urban II offered the first plenary indulgence, that is one giving remission from *all* suffering in purgatory, to those who confessed their sins and 'took the cross'. Yet if crusaders, who were armed pilgrims, could receive a plenary indulgence, why not their brothers who carried no more than a wooden staff? The Franciscans claimed the first such papal plenary indulgence for those who visited their shrine of the Portiuncula long before it was officially granted to them in 1294. Once the precedent had been established, the Pope offered another plenary indulgence to pilgrims coming to Rome in the jubilee year of 1300. Meanwhile the custodians of most other shrines sought from their bishop or from Rome partial indulgences, and the price they had to pay steadily rose as the decades passed. Eventually many local shrines also acquired the right to offer indulgences associated with more famous shrines, thereby drawing to themselves pilgrims who saw no point in making a long, hazardous and expensive journey overseas for spiritual benefits which could be obtained in the next shire.

The sale of indulgences developed from small beginnings in the twelfth century. A man too old or infirm to go on crusade received permission to send a substitute, and could still claim the benefits of the plenary indulgence. In like manner it came to be accepted that a substitute pilgrim could be hired, either by an ailing person or by his relatives after his death. It became common for men to make provision in their wills for payment to be made so that a pilgrim could journey to pray at a shrine for the soul of the departed person. The same principle lay behind the foundation of chantry chapels, where masses for the departed were daily offered. Just as would-be crusaders were eventually allowed to send money rather than a replacement, so gradually money payments for indulgences proved to be an acceptable alternative either to doing penance in person or to hiring a stand-in. In the later Middle Ages pardoners appeared on the scene selling indulgences on more attractive terms than those obtainable at the local shrines, not unlike their modern secular counterparts, the door-to-door insurance salesmen.

Many other motives besides the desire for forgiveness drew pilgrims to the holy places. In an age where medical science remained rudimentary the blind, halt and lame stumbled towards the shrines of the saints hoping for the not uncommon healing miracles. Indeed it could be said that the saints were regarded as the senior consultants of medieval medical practice. Other pilgrims journeyed to Jerusalem or Rome, Santiago or Trier, or to their native shrines, for devotional reasons. To them the relics they saw and touched seemed to bridge the gap between their tangible, material and temporal existence and the unseen, spiritual world of heaven. For the greater number of people whose concrete and practical minds were little inclined towards the abstractions of theology and contemplation, relics brought them closer to the historical Jesus and the saints of the heroic period: their imaginations could feed upon these holy objects as surely as their souls received nourishment from the Body and Blood of Christ. Moreover, a pilgrimage could be *done*: it was devotion pitched in the language of action rather than belief.

Although theologians such as Thomas Aquinas could justify the veneration of saints and their relics, neither it nor the associated practice of pilgrimage ever belonged to the essentials of Christian duty (in contrast to Islam, where pilgrimage to Mecca is an obligation laid on all believers). Pilgrimage was fundamentally a popular and spontaneous expression of feeling and need, which the Church strove to control. At various times and places we shall find the Church authorities encouraging and capitalizing upon pilgrimage, merely tolerating it or even actively trying to prohibit certain forms of it, such as resort to unauthorized holy wells and, in later ages, the graves of uncanonized local saints.

The popular nature of pilgrimage creates particular problems for the historian. The common folk of the Middle Ages have not left us much first-hand evidence about their thoughts and emotions, not least because most of them were illiterate. Between about the third century and the Reformation in the sixteenth century several millions of men, women and children made one or more pilgrimages in Britain or beyond the seas, and yet we lack all but a few eye-witness accounts of what it was like to be a pilgrim. Therefore the historian has to assemble his picture from surviving documents, traditions, buildings and artefacts, not unlike those antiquarians who reassembled the shrine of St Alban from several thousand fragments into which the original had been shattered by the hammers of Tudor workmen during the Reformation. We should constantly remind ourselves of how little we know about the real medieval pilgrims.

Some historians have attempted to divide the history of medieval pilgrimage into chronological periods, but its popular character militates against such compartments. What can be seen in the late Middle Ages is the way in which the basic ideas or themes implicit in the practice were developed as far as they could go, so that their full-blown forms strained the credulity of intelligent contemporaries. Certainly the numbers of pilgrims on English roads appears to have gradually declined in the fourteenth and fifteenth centuries. Moreover, as Chaucer's *Canterbury Tales* (written between *c.* 1380 and 1400) suggests, pilgrimages had become for many largely an outward empty form disguising a colourful variety of what we would now call secular motives: travel, holidays and a good time. In the late fourteenth century critics of such pilgrimages appeared among the people in the heretics known as the Lollards – those first-fruits of the English Reformation. But the history of pilgrimage merely mirrors the growth, flowering and decline of medieval Christianity as a whole.

Thus parts of the tree of medieval pilgrimage had become rotten long before the Reformers laid their axes to it. But other branches, nurtured by roots deep in the soil of religious human nature, were very much alive. In a much attenuated form, Christian pilgrimage in Britain survived the Reformation, and even put forth new branches as Catholicism slowly regained its foothold, both through the survival, growth and eventual restoration of the Roman Catholic Church and through the conversion of a part of the established Church of England to Anglo-Catholicism in the nineteenth century. Meanwhile, in the Protestant fledgling tradition, the idea of pilgrimage – pruned of all externals – remained a powerful image of the Christian life, as John Bunyan would so triumphantly reveal. Even in our more secular century pilgrims can still be found at such places as Shakespeare's birthplace, or filing past the intact body of Lenin in Moscow. Like their medieval counterparts they are seeking to express devotion and to bridge that ever-widening gap between the present and the past.

Base of the shrine of St Bertram or Bertelin, a local saint, in the church at Ilam, Staffordshire. Upon it would have stood a canopy decorated with figures. Holes or niches were a common feature (see, for instance, pp. 53, 76, 139): they allowed pilgrims to get as close as possible to the heart of the shrine.

THE SOUTH-EAST

1 Aylesford, Kent, seen across the River Medway. The fourteenth-century bridge is believed to have been built by monks from the Carmelite priory – which itself possed a saint's relics – primarily for the use of pilgrims on their way to Canterbury (see p. 58).

2 One scene from a healing miracle recounted in stained glass of about 1220 in the Trinity Chapel of Canterbury Cathedral, where St Thomas Becket's shrine stood: a boy cured by the miraculous Water of St Thomas, brought by pilgrims. (For the rest of the story, see p. 41.)

3 The Corona, a unique circular chapel at the east end of Canterbury Cathedral, built to house the reliquary of St Thomas Becket's 'Crown', the thin saucer of bone cut from his skull at his martyrdom. His successors are enthroned as archbishops of Canterbury in 'St Augustine's Chair', made of Purbeck marble, which probably dates from the early thirteenth century.

THE WEST

4 Glastonbury Tor in Somerset, crowned by the fifteenth-century tower of St Michael's Chapel, which was one of the stations visited by pilgrims. Like many hills and mountains – including St Michael's Mount, opposite – on the coming of Christianity the Tor was dedicated to the Archangel.

5 St Michael's Mount, Cornwall. Here, according to legend, storm-tossed fishermen had a vision of the Archangel.

THE EAST

6 Walsingham. The ruined east window, in the distance, stood at the end of the priory church. The base of one side of the west door can be seen in the foreground. Note the decorated panels filled with split flints, characteristic of East Anglia. The church was 244 feet long.

7 Ely Cathedral from the south. The medieval houses below the great west tower belong to the cathedral and choir school.

THE MIDLANDS

8 Reliquary of a bone of St Chad in a chapel in the north-west part of St Chad's Cathedral, Birmingham. Other reputed relics of the Saint are in a casket above the high altar.

9 Lincoln Cathedral from the south-west. The home of several shrines in the Middle Ages, it still dominates the city below it.

THE WELSH MARCHES AND WALES

10 Holy Cross Church, Mwnt, with 'The Mount' behind it. The original church is thought to have been a halting place for pilgrims on their way to Bardsey (p. 166), and it may have served also as a mortuary chapel where the bodies of saints being taken to Bardsey for burial rested for a time.

11 St Beuno's Church, Pistyll. According to one tradition the Saint's bones rest beneath the altar. A hospice for pilgrims to Bardsey stood nearby.

SCOTLAND

12 Cloth or 'Cloutie' Well at Culloden, showing the votive 'clouts' hanging from neighbouring trees. Although far more common in Ireland, there are a number of these wells in the district around Inverness.

13 The Monymusk Reliquary or *Brecbennoch*. This unique portable shrine of late seventh- or early eighth-century date may have housed a relic of St Columba. Ornamented in silver and gold, it is small enough (only 4⅛ inches across) to have been hung on a chain around someone's neck. (National Museum of Antiquities of Scotland, Edinburgh)

14 The medieval abbey of Iona, much restored in modern times, stands on the site of St Columba's early monastic settlement.

15 St Ninian's Cave, Whithorn. An eighth-century poem written at Whithorn refers to the Saint withdrawing to a *horrendum antrum*, 'an awesome cavern'. The traditional cave fits that description, as this view from the desolate beach reveals.

IRELAND

16 The shrine of the head of St Oliver Plunkett in St Peter's Church at Drogheda, County Louth. He was martyred at Tyburn in 1681 and canonized in 1975.

17 St Manchan's Reliquary, in the church at Boher, County Offaly. The twelfth-century tomb-shaped shrine, made of wood ornamented with bronze, gilt and enamel, is an important example of the craftsmanship which flourished during the Irish revival after the end of the Viking raids.

18 The Rock of Cashel. The core of the buildings on the citadel is the roofless thirteenth-century cathedral, with the bishop's castle at its west end (right). Attached to it are two earlier buildings, a tenth-century round tower and Cormac's Chapel (see p. 196), of which the two low towers can be seen beyond the ruins of the cathedral choir.

19 Our Lady's Island, County Wexford, looking out across the waters of the lake towards the sea. Pilgrims have come here for centuries, especially on the Feast of the Assumption (15 August).

THE NORTH

20 St Cuthbert, depicted as a bishop in a wall-painting of about 1200 in the Galilee Chapel of Durham Cathedral.

VOX PATRIS
VIS MARTIRIS

9

12

13

14

15

BEATO OLIVERO SACRUM

20

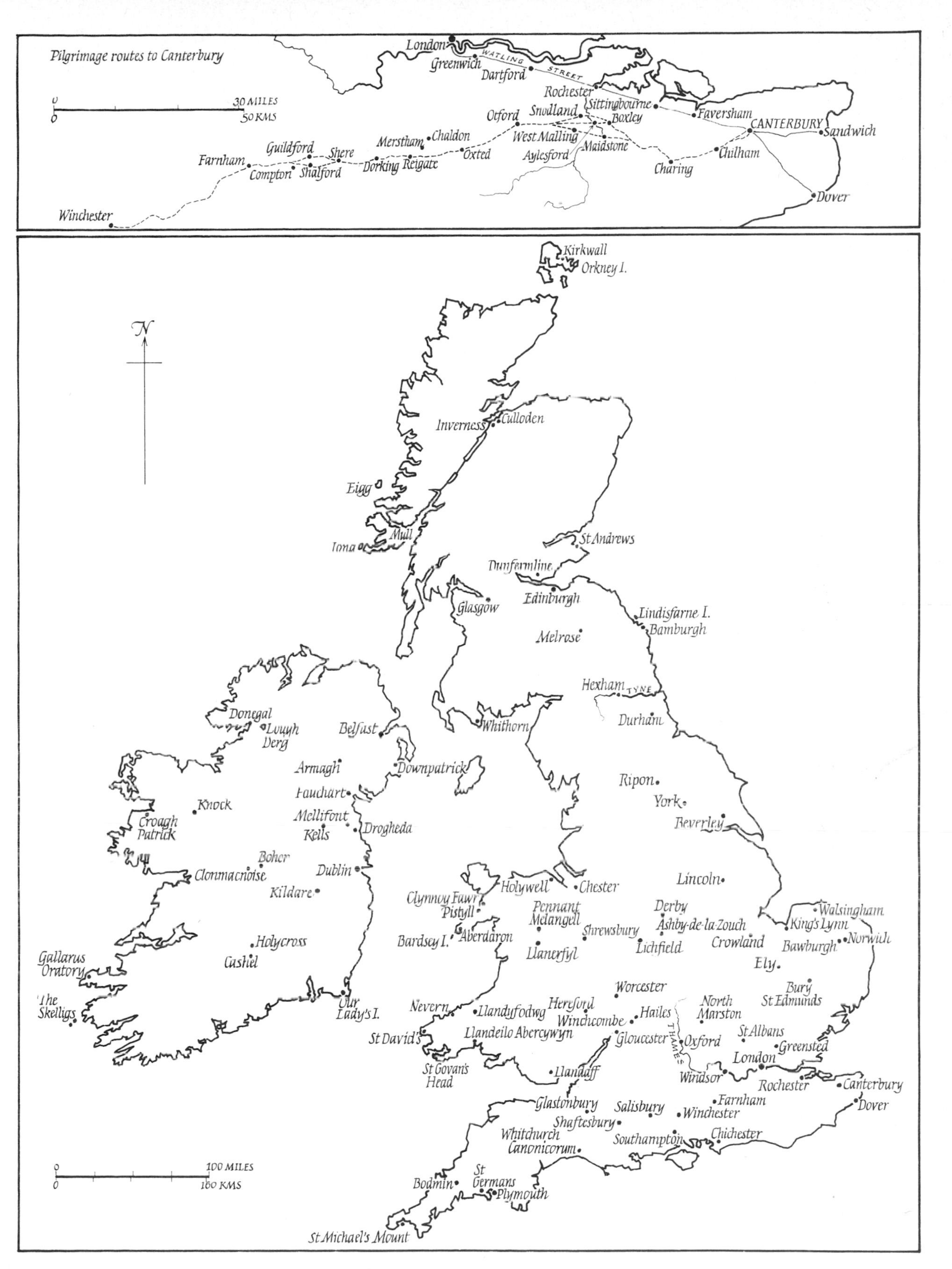
Pilgrimage routes to Canterbury
30 MILES
50 KMS
London
Greenwich
WATLING STREET
Dartford
Rochester
Sittingbourne
Faversham
CANTERBURY
Sandwich
Otford
Snodland
Boxley
West Malling
Maidstone
Aylesford
Chilham
Charing
Dover
Merstham
Chaldon
Oxted
Dorking
Reigate
Guildford
Shere
Farnham
Compton
Shalford
Winchester
Kirkwall
Orkney I.
N
Inverness
Culloden
Eigg
Mull
Iona
St Andrews
Dunfermline
Edinburgh
Glasgow
Lindisfarne I.
Bamburgh
Melrose
Hexham
TYNE
Durham
Whithorn
Donegal
Lough Derg
Belfast
Armagh
Downpatrick
Faughart
Knock
Mellifont
Croagh Patrick
Kells
Drogheda
Boher
Clonmacnoise
Dublin
Kildare
Holycross
Cashel
Gallarus Oratory
The Skelligs
Our Lady's I.
Ripon
York
Beverley
Lincoln
Holywell
Chester
Clynnog Fawr
Pistyll
Pennant Melangell
Derby
Ashby-de-la-Zouch
Shrewsbury
Lichfield
Crowland
Walsingham
King's Lynn
Bawburgh
Norwich
Ely
Bardsey I.
Aberdaron
Llanerfyl
Worcester
Bury St Edmunds
Nevern
Llandyfodwg
Hereford
Winchcombe
Hailes
North Marston
St David's
Llandeilo Abercywyn
Gloucester
THAMES
Oxford
St Albans
Greensted
London
St Govan's Head
Llandaff
Windsor
Rochester
Canterbury
Glastonbury
Salisbury
Farnham
Winchester
Dover
Shaftesbury
Whitchurch Canonicorum
Southampton
Chichester
100 MILES
160 KMS
Bodmin
St Germans
Plymouth
St Michael's Mount

The South-East

Canterbury *St Thomas Becket*

THE 'HOLY BLISSFUL MARTYR'

When the sweet showers of April fall and shoot
Down through the drought of March to pierce the root,
Bathing every vein in liquid power
From which there springs the engendering of the flower . . .
Then people long to go on pilgrimages
And palmers long to seek the stranger strands
Of far-off saints, hallowed in sundry lands,
And specially, from every shire's end
In England, down to Canterbury they wend
To seek the holy blissful martyr, quick
In giving help to them when they were sick.

Chaucer, *The Canterbury Tales*, c. 1380–1400

No other name in the history of pilgrimage in Britain can compare with that of St Thomas Becket. His martyrdom and canonization formed the essential preliminaries to centuries of posthumous fame. We can only understand the peculiar lure of Canterbury if we first recapture the events which gave rise to it, that story which every pilgrim would recreate in his own mind as he knelt at each 'station' of the martyrdom in Canterbury Cathedral. Fortunately a number of contemporary accounts have survived, mainly by monks who either saw the events for themselves or took down the reports of eye-witnesses. Their vividness allows us to feel the force of Becket's personality and the shock of his death.

The cathedral where Becket ruled and died was almost entirely different from the building that we see today (the choir was rebuilt soon after his death, the rest in the late Middle Ages); and because the accounts are so circumstantial it is important that we know what it was like. Its massive nave and transepts, built by the first Norman archbishop after the Conquest, were then some hundred years old; the transepts were unusual in having each a central pillar that supported an upper gallery. East of the transepts, and reached from them by flights of steps, was a splendid new choir, raised high over a crypt dedicated to the Virgin (which survives today). At the easternmost end of the great church was the Trinity Chapel, which was to be specially associated with Becket (see p. 68).

Thomas Becket, son of an immigrant Norman merchant domiciled in London, is said to have trained as a knight at Pevensey Castle, but he subsequently entered the household of Theobald, Archbishop of Canterbury. After further studies abroad and some diplomatic service in Rome he became (after ordination as deacon) Archdeacon of Canterbury. On Theobald's suggestion, King Henry II made him his Chancellor. His working relationship with Henry – fifteen years his junior – grew into friendship, and in 1162 Thomas became Archbishop of Canterbury.

The celebrated quarrel between the two friends began with Becket's resolute opposition to the imposition of any limits on the rights of the clergy to be tried in their own courts and under their own laws. This issue became the gauntlet in a power struggle not only between Church and State in England but also between the English Crown and the Papacy. For some years Becket pursued his case in exile abroad. After a reconciliation he returned home, but another difficult issue had arisen during his absence. Henry had caused his son to be crowned King, not merely as his successor but also as his co-regent. Becket felt incensed, because the holder of his office alone should have performed such a ceremony. He procured from the Pope a suspension of the Archbishop of York and a revival of former excommunications for the Bishops of London and Salisbury, the participants in the coronation service.

These three prelates found King Henry near Bayeux in Normandy. During their audience with him one anonymous voice declared: 'As long as Thomas lives, you will have neither good days, nor peaceful kingdom, nor quiet life.' The florid, red-haired Henry fell into one of those paroxysms of fury to which all the early Plantagenets were prone: his brow furrowed, his face became red, and his eyes rolled and flashed. His railing tone against Becket became suddenly challenging. 'What sluggard wretches!' he roared at his silent and apprehensive courtiers. 'What cowards have I brought up in my court who care nothing for their allegiance to their master! Not one will deliver me from this low-born priest!'; and with these fatal words he rushed out of the hall.

Among the court that day stood four knights named Reginald FitzUrse, Hugh de Morville, William de Tracy and Richard le Bret. They rode all night by different routes to the French coast and reached a rendezvous next day (27 December 1170) at Saltwood Castle, near Hythe, some fourteen miles from Canterbury. On the following morning they issued orders for a troop of men-at-arms to be raised in the neighbourhood, and then rode up the Roman road called Stone Street to Canterbury, where they made their way to St Augustine's Abbey just outside the walls (see p. 66). Although the monks of that house sided with Becket in his quarrel the Abbot was no friend of the Archbishop and he received them. Having issued a proclamation forbidding any citizen of Canterbury to assist Becket, the four knights remounted and with a dozen others rode beside the walls until they reached the great gateway to the Archbishop's palace.

The 'Pilgrims' Way' to Canterbury above Boxley Abbey in Kent (see p. 59).

Miniature at the head of John of Salisbury's early account of Becket's murder. Late twelfth-century in date, it may be the oldest surviving picture of the martyrdom. Above, Becket is shown in the hall, with the knights outside in the courtyard. Below, monks hide in the cathedral as the fatal blow is struck. (British Library, London, Cotton MS Claudius B.ii)

Meanwhile on that fateful day, Tuesday 29 December, Becket had followed his normal daily routine of Mass, business in the chapter-house and the receipt – as seems to have been his custom – of three scourgings. At three o'clock he sat down to a dinner of roast pheasant in the palace hall, drinking more than usual. After dinner and the concluding Latin hymn he went to his room and sat on his bed talking to his household staff. In the hall a crowd of beggars and paupers had swarmed inside to sit on the benches or squat upon the fresh hay and straw which had been placed for them on the floor, finishing up the remains of the feast. When they were finally turned out into the cold courtyard at about four-thirty they may have noticed the four knights, gowns and cloaks hiding their mail armour, dismount and enter the hall.

An usher led the Norman knights into the presence of the tall, spare, fifty-three year-old Primate of All England, who at first pretended to ignore them. They poured out the complaints of the King against him, only to be met by contradictions and counter-accusations. The knights, we are told, were working themselves into a passion: shouting, jumping to their feet, thrusting their heads closer to him, twisting their long gloves, and gesticulating violently. Becket, thoroughly aroused, whipped them with his sharp tongue. Seeing the throng of servants and clergy which had now gathered in the room, the four knights left the chamber exclaiming 'It is you who threaten.'

Passing through the hall and court they cried 'To arms! To arms!' The gateway was seized and the oak doors slammed shut. Under a sycamore tree in the garden the knights threw off their cloaks and gowns, and strapped on their swords. As the hall door had been barred against them they ran to the orchard at the back, where a stairway led up to the antechamber linking the hall and Becket's bedroom. The carpenters repairing the wooden steps had left their tools behind, and FitzUrse seized an axe, mounted the steps and broke his way through an oriel window.

Hearing the violent commotion outside, the companions of the Archbishop urged him to seek safety in the cathedral. Vespers were due to begin shortly at five o'clock, and the Archbishop, in white surplice under a brown cloak edged with white wool, set out behind his cross-bearer. Instead of following the usual route through the orchard to the west door of the cathedral they made their way into the monastery cloister, where his frightened attendants pulled and pushed him ever faster towards the door of the north transept. Vespers had already begun in the candle-lit choir, but the noise in the cloister caused half the monks to abandon their prayers and to hide in the aisles. By now the knights were rallying their followers in the cloister, driving back a crowd of terrified servants to the north door which Becket had mercifully ordered to be opened for them. Once inside, these fugitives scattered with all but three of the Archbishop's companions into the shadows of the cathedral. Hard on their heels the knights entered the church.

The light had almost faded from the north transept, but they caught sight of a group of clergy beyond the central pillar clustered around some steps in the aisle leading up towards the high altar. FitzUrse, holding sword in one hand and carpenter's axe in the other, ran forward to the right of the pillar and the other three went round it on the left. One called out 'Stay!'; another, 'Where is Thomas Becket, traitor to the King?' Becket, who was on the fourth step, turned and revealed his face. The knights attempted to drag him out of the cathedral so that no sacrilege would be committed, but Becket struggled to avoid it. He put his back to the central pillar and wrestled with the knights and their assistants, seizing William de Tracy by his coat-of-mail and hurling him to the stone pavement with words of abuse. FitzUrse closed upon him, bellowing in Norman-French '*Ferez! Ferez!*' – 'Strike! Strike!' – but his sword blow merely dislodged the Archbishop's cap. De Tracy leapt forward and struck hard, but a Saxon monk called Edward Grim (who later wrote an account of the murder), had his arm round Becket and threw it up, wrapped in a cloak, to parry the blade, though the spent force of it grazed the Archbishop's head and cut his left shoulder. Another blow from Tracy stunned him and he fell in front of the eastern wall of the transept near the aisle. Richard le Bret struck next with such violence that his sword sliced off the top of Becket's skull, and shattered into two pieces on the flagstone. Finally one of the company, taunted for hanging back, completed the bloody business by planting his foot on the neck of the corpse, and thrusting his sword into the skull so that brains were scattered in the spreading pool of blood. 'Let us go,' he said: 'the traitor is dead; he will rise no more.'

The murderers, excited or relieved that the deed was done, ran shouting as in battle *'Reaux! Reaux!'* – 'The King's Men! The King's Men!' – through the cloisters and into the palace, which they proceeded to ransack. As they rode off into the night on Becket's horses, their saddlebags bulging with gold and silver plate, documents and papal bulls, a great storm filled the skies with peals of angry thunder, flashes of lightning and a downpour of heavy rain.

In the darkness the monks eventually summoned up their courage and returned to the corpse. They carefully gathered the discarded weapons, dressed the gaping head, and collected up blood and brains in bowls. Bystanders cut off pieces of cloth from their gowns, dipped them in the blood and anointed their eyes. Afterwards the clergy carried the body to a spot before the high altar where it rested that night with basins under the bier to catch any drops of falling blood. Here the monks discovered beneath the many layers of clothes on the corpse a monastic habit and rough haircloth underclothes unwashed and seething with lice. Realizing that the somewhat secular Archbishop had been one of them all along (though it is possible that Becket had donned the thick monastic habit along with other extra clothes as protection either against the cold or against the expected attack), the monks burst into songs of thanksgiving and kissed the hands and feet of the corpse, hailing him as 'Saint Thomas!' Arnold, a monk who was goldsmith to the monastery, led a party back to the spot where Becket fell in order to scrape up the remaining blood and brains, and to fence the area with benches. A citizen of Canterbury in the now thronged cathedral dipped the corner of his shirt in the blood and gave it, mixed with water, to his paralysed wife at home, who was said to have been cured. Later the monks attired the body in the consecration clothes of the Archbishop and the insignia of his office, taking off the ring set with a green stone he had been wearing. Fearful of an attempt to steal the body, they buried it in the crypt.

Some of the monks had immediately embarked for Rome to convey their version of the story to the Pope. Within a year Alexander III sent legates to investigate the miracles associated with Thomas Becket: they carried back with them such relics as the blood-stained tunic and a fragment of the flagstone bearing bloodstains. In 1173 the Pope officially canonized Becket, making 29 December the Feast of St Thomas of Canterbury.

When King Henry heard news of the murder he shut himself up for three days, ate nothing except almonds and milk, donned sackcloth and ashes, and frequently shouted out that he was not accountable for the crime. Europe did not absolve him from all blame, and he could not ignore even if he had wanted to the general outcry against the deed. On his return from campaigning in Ireland in 1172 he made his first public penance in Normandy. At a council afterwards he swore again his innocence, made restitution in the matters of dispute with the dead Saint, and offered to go on a three-year pilgrimage to the Holy Land or St James of Compostela, and supply two hundred men-at-arms for service with the Knights Templar. Such professions of penitence, however, did not prevent him from receiving for a while half the valuble gifts offered at the martyred Archbishop's tomb.

Two years later, faced with the rebellion of his sons, an invasion from Scotland and general revolt in the shires, Henry hastened back from his campaigns in Normandy and arrived at Southampton in July 1174. Living on a penitential diet of bread and water he rode to Canterbury, probably along what is known now as the 'Pilgrims' Way' (see pp. 33, 55–65). At Harbledown, where it joined the London road, he halted and ordained a gift of twenty marks a year to the leper-house or hospital. (Today, after eight centuries, the gift – valued at £13.33 – is still paid by the Crown to the Harbledown almshouses.) Once in sight of the three towers of the cathedral he dismounted and continued on foot to St Dunstan's Church on the city outskirts, where he stripped off his clothes and put on the hair shirt and woollen dress of a penitential pilgrim. Barefoot and cloaked against the rain, he walked through the streets to the cathedral.

Having knelt at the porch the King went straight to the north transept where he fell to his knees again and with tears in his eyes kissed the stone where Becket had collapsed. In the crypt he knelt groaning and weeping before the tomb while Bishop Foliot of London pointed out to the congregation his evident penitence and described his gift of forty marks a year to keep candles burning perpetually before the Martyr's resting place. After standing up to ratify

The penance of Henry II. An early fifteenth-century roof boss in the cloister of Norwich Cathedral shows the monks of Canterbury beating the bared back of the King as he kneels before Becket's tomb.

what had been said, Henry received absolution from the Bishop and a kiss of reconciliation from the Prior. Kneeling once more, he removed the cloak but retained the woollen shirt which covered the hair shirt, and, placing his head and shoulders through one of the apertures in the tomb (see p. 39), received five strokes of the rod from every bishop and abbot present and three from every monk. Now absolved, he dressed but remained all night in the crypt leaning against one of the pillars, his bare feet on the cold flagstones. After morning devotions around the cathedral he finally drank from the Martyr's Well, and left for London carrying away with him some phials of the water mixed with the blood of St Thomas.

These spiritual exertions sent the King to his sick bed in the capital, but tidings soon arrived that his forces had captured the King of Scotland on the very day of his penance. Alnwick Castle had fallen to him, and contrary winds foiled a Flemish fleet bent upon invasion, so that his sons could not sustain the war against him. Having so manifestly proved his goodwill, the Martyr-Saint henceforth enjoyed the royal patronage.

By an irony of history one of the causes for which Becket stood – namely that laymen who murdered priests should only be tried by clerical courts – meant that his murderers could not be punished with more than excommunication. Monkish and popular imagination painted horrible fates in various legends for the four knights, but the real facts are not so dramatic. One of them certainly attempted a pilgrimage to Jerusalem. Within two years they were all back in court, hunting or hawking with their royal master. Morville seems to have flourished in the north under King John, while FitzUrse probably settled in Ireland. The village of Sanford Bret in Somerset owes its name to the family of the third conspirator. Not four years after the murder William de Tracy, who had struck the first and second blows, held the high office of Justiciar of Normandy, and he remained powerful in the West Country of England where most of his lands lay. But he made over to Canterbury Cathedral the manor of Dockham in Devonshire 'for the love of God, and the salvation of his own soul and his ancestors, and for the love of the blessed Thomas Archbishop and Martyr', in order to provide clothing and support for one monk to celebrate masses for the souls of the living and dead.

THE FIRST CANTERBURY PILGRIMS

Within days of the martyrdom of St Thomas pilgrims from the towns and countryside near Canterbury began to converge on the cathedral, the first streams which swelled into a mighty river of pilgrims. The wonderful efficacy of the Saint's entombed body and the few drops of his blood mixed with gallons of water – the famous Water of St Thomas – drew invalids towards them like iron filings attracted to a magnet. Soon a monk called Benedict, who had heard the sounds of Becket's murder as he hid inside the cathedral, received directions to act as custodian of the relics and to minister to the sick folk whom he described as 'lying in pain all about the church'. Later a more credulous monk called William was appointed to act as his colleague. William had also heard the knights enter the cathedral, but when FitzUrse bellowed 'Strike! Strike!' he fled away and justified himself later on the grounds that he felt no call to be a martyr. From Benedict's record of the miracles performed by St Thomas in the first year after his death we are able to identify some of the earliest Canterbury pilgrims by name, and to catch a glimpse of their humanity.

The news of Becket's murder certainly travelled fast. Two days later, the wife of a Sussex knight prayed to St Thomas and experienced a miraculous cure. On Saturday a Gloucester girl found that her head pains had gone after she invoked the Martyr, while on the following day the swollen arm of William Belet, knight of Enborne in Berkshire, resumed its normal size.

It is no wonder that pilgrims hearing such stories hastened to the tomb at Canterbury. Robert, a smith of Thanet, blind for two years, received his sight back that first Whitsuntide after the martyrdom: three medallions of stained glass in the rebuilt Trinity Chapel, where the shrine later stood, depict the cure and his subsequent offering of a large bowl of gold pieces in gratitude. Mad Henry of Fordwich, dragged by his friends struggling and shouting to the tomb of St Thomas and left there all night, recovered his senses. Two servants of the elderly and paralysed Sir William of Dene supported their master in the saddle, one walking on each side, but thanks to his miraculous cure he returned home on foot leaving his crutches at the tomb. A lady called Saxera of Dover slept by the tomb all night and dreamt that St Thomas appeared to her saying 'Rise, offer thy candle.' When she awoke her intestinal complaint had disappeared. Richard, son of Walter, a scholar of Northampton, who had endured diarrhoea and liver trouble for nine years, arrived in a carriage but walked away from Canterbury completely cured.

Soon after Easter 1171 the monks heard whispers of a threat to remove the wonder-working body, and so they encased it in the crypt below the Trinity Chapel in a plain, low outer tomb of veined marble pierced with two large holes on each side so that pilgrims could reach through and touch the coffin. These holes were a feature in many shrines, and we shall encounter them again. They existed to allow direct contact with the actual wood or stone which held the relics and was thus considered to be more holy than the outer structure, however magnificent the latter may have been. Once an agile madman wormed his way into one of the holes and lay inside the casing with his head at the Martyr's feet and his feet near St Thomas's head. While the monks debated whether or not to break the shrine open with hammers he miraculously emerged again. Neither he nor a lithe youth could repeat the extraordinary performance.

After Whitsuntide the miracles continued. As soon as Matilda and Roger resolved to have their sick illegitimate infant 'measured for a candle' the Saint saved its life, a story which illustrates the widespread practice of offering a candle of the same height, length or weight as the supplicant to burn at a saint's shrine. Gilbert, a London shoemaker with a fistula, after a draught of the miraculous Water walked home in a day (some sixty-six miles), and then stripped to the waist and challenged his neighbours to a foot race. The Prior of St Frideswide's at Oxford wrote to Benedict certifying that he had himself been cured by the Water. A knight, bidden by the Saint in a dream to go on pilgrimage with the words 'Fail not to do this, whether it please thy wife or displease her', felt his health beginning to return as he neared Canterbury. He spent the night in the cathedral, the pains in his legs growing worse. Then he offered to the Saint two waxen legs the same size as his own, and after making his confession next morning he found the pain had disappeared. Solomon of London, nearly a century old and blind for six years, saw again after spending a night in prayer at the tomb.

The Saint could be vindictive to those who deceived him or showed disrespect to his relics. He struck blind a man who had been pretending to be blind. Two boys who fell asleep at his shrine leaning their heads upon it returned home unhealed. An impious person frequently found his pyx of Water mysteriously emptied before he had taken many steps from the cathedral. These early wooden boxes or pyxes containing the 'blood' of the 'Lamb of Canterbury', some with mirrors fitted inside the lids for lady pilgrims, tended to leak anyway. Earthenware broke too easily, so the townsfolk used cast lead

A thirteenth-century lead ampulla *for the Water of St Thomas, inscribed in Latin 'Thomas is the best healer of the holy sick'. (Museum of London)*

or tin phials. These *ampullae*, usually hung around the neck, became one of the more popular badges or tokens of the Canterbury pilgrimage, just as the scallop-shell served for St James of Compostela and the palm-leaf for Jerusalem.

Grateful pilgrims often left some visible sign of their cure at the shrine. Henry, son of an Essex knight, who suffered for several years 'as though his intestines were being cut with razors', drank the Water. At first it seemed to make his condition worse, but then it caused him to cough up a worm longer than a man's hand. This the youth hung up near the shrine for the edification of other pilgrims.

What did it feel like to drink the wonder-working Water of St Thomas? John, chaplain to the Archdeacon of Salop, troubled by a painful polypus in his nose which eventually began to cause paralysis, described the sensation of the Water, cold as ice, chasing the disease through his body and almost freezing his brain. After enduring this internal torture John gave a mighty sneeze and then found a cherry-stone in his mouth. He got up and walked home quite healed, but stoutly refused to leave the cherry-stone behind – his precious evidence of a divine intervention in his life.

Some sick pilgrims found their condition alleviated rather than cured. Godiva of Chelmsford, five years blind, 'falling before the Martyr's tomb, saw the sunlight, and could discern bodies and colours, but she did not receive her sight perfectly', wrote Benedict. Other cures worked gradually, not without assistance from the monks. Eda of Scotland arrived at Canterbury in a litter having been bed-ridden for ten years. After passing three days and nights near the tomb she drank the Water. Roger, one of the custodian monks, bade her to come to him. 'How can I?' she replied. 'In the name of the Martyr, I bid you rise and come to me', commanded Roger. That day she could walk on tip-toe around the tomb, and the following day she placed her whole weight on the soles of her feet. Later, Eda returned on horseback to her native Scotland.

Faith and persistence could help the Saint to work miracles in difficult cases. Godwin of Brithwell in Yorkshire spent some days in Canterbury before going homewards as lame as ever. On his way he saw a vision of Thomas exhorting him to return to the tomb and to pray more earnestly. At first he intended to disregard the invitation, but two Yorkshire knights whom he met next day persuaded him to go back in their company to Canterbury. He slept another night with his head at the Martyr's feet and regained the normal use of his limbs.

The influence of the Saint could thus work at a distance. In 1171 the townsfolk fished Robert, a boy of Rochester, out of the Medway. He looked blue and lifeless. When they hung him upside down no water came out, nor could they make him vomit by rolling him in a tub. From three o'clock to Vespers he lay in this condition until his mother measured him and promised St Thomas an equal length of silver thread if the boy recovered – which he promptly did. The opening scenes of this miracle are vividly depicted in three medallions of stained glass in a window in the Trinity Chapel (sixth from the west on the north side of the site of the shrine). In the first medallion the boys are seen on the banks of the Medway pelting frogs in the reeds with sticks and stones while the son tumbles in the river. In the second scene the boys tell the tidings to the parents at the door of their house. In the third, the parents are shown on the river bank gazing with grief on the corpse of their son being pulled out of the water.

In the same window, nine more medallions recount a succession of miracles concerning a knight called Jordan FitzEisulf, who lived at Pontefract. Sickness killed his young son's nurse and then the boy himself. That day, however, twenty pilgrims from Canterbury lodged in the house. Sir Jordan received from them some of the Water of St Thomas and forced it down the boy's throat. After a third draught the son opened his eyes and spoke. Jordan put into the boy's hands four pieces of silver to be an offering to the Martyr before mid-Lent. But the vow was forgotten, and St Thomas

The story of Sir Jordan FitzEisulf, in the stained glass of the Trinity Chapel in Canterbury Cathedral, about 1220. In the bottom left corner the funeral of the first victim, the nurse, is depicted. Next to it is the death of Sir Jordan's son William, followed by the arrival of the pilgrims with the Water of St Thomas (see colour plate 2). In the top left corner Jordan's wife gives him coins which he places in the child's hands as a votive offering. Next, the child sits up and eats while the parents give thanks. In the top right corner St Thomas appears to the leper Gimp, who is shown greeting the parents in the next medallion (centre row, left). Ignoring his message they see their eldest son die. Finally, the vow at last accomplished, Jordan is shown emptying coins at the Saint's tomb, accompanied by his wife and their boy.

appeared to one Gimp, a leper living three miles away, to go and warn Sir Jordan of the consequences. Hearing the warning, Jordan fixed the last weeks in Lent for his pilgrimage, but a visit from the Lord Warden of the Cinque Ports put it out of his mind. Sudden sickness then struck down the household, and Jordan's eldest son died on the Friday after Easter. Themselves ill but sustained by the holy Water, Jordan and his wife set off to pay their vow. She fainted seven times on the first day. At the sight of the towers of Canterbury Cathedral she dismounted and with her husband and remaining son walked barefoot, carrying pilgrim staves, to seek the saving forgiveness of the Martyr. Among the glass medallions vividly portraying this story there is one showing the first death-bed scene, with Jordan pouring the wonder-working fluid through the boy's clenched teeth while the pilgrims gaze on, each holding his staff and bottle of Water of St Thomas.

People gave thanks-offerings to St Thomas for a variety of services, far short of the miracle of raising the dead, such as recovering a missing loaf or surviving an ordeal by boiling water or winning a lawsuit. Radulph the Fleming tied a coin to the broken leg of his daughter and vowed an annual payment if it set correctly. Another Fleming, who offered a silver coin if he caught a hawk that had eluded capture for eight days, secured the bird and paid his due to St Thomas. The owner of a lost horse found him after promising to present a wax figure of the animal at the shrine of St Thomas. A pilgrim on his way home was caught in the great fire of Rochester in 1177 and found himself repulsed at every door until the servant of Gilbert the Baker gave him refuge from the blazing inferno of the street. He leapt up to the roof, took out his phial of Water, fixed it to the end of a pole and drove back the flames which threatened to engulf the house.

Sometimes the penance of making any pilgrimage included receiving a certain number of strokes with a rod at the Saint's tomb. Henry II, it will be recalled, bared his back for such a punishment. The monks who acted as custodians probably administered this part of the penance, either in public or behind an altar or in a side chapel. In later times especially the blows may have fallen lightly and served more as tokens of a beating than the real thing. But the same Trinity Chapel window depicts in one scene a kneeling woman bowing herself to the ground before a priest at an altar who is taking from her a large candle. Two men with long rods – possibly the two lay assistants to the custodians – who are standing by can be seen in the next frame plying their sticks to good effect upon her. In a third compartment of the window she falls fainting to the ground while one of them continues to beat her. The priest is reading from a book, presumably a penitential Psalm, while a pilgrim with his staff watches the flagellation with much concern: perhaps it was his turn next.

Occasionally the stories collected by Benedict, and subsequently his colleague William, give us glimpses of pilgrims actually on the road. A pilgrim from the

Two further stories from the same window. The top three medallions tell the story of Robert, the Rochester boy: (1) he falls face first into the Medway where he had been trying to catch frogs, one of whom watches the rescue; (2) two of his companions tell his parents; (3) they weep as Robert is fished out of the river more dead than alive.

The three medallions in the bottom row show a maniac (probably the murderess Matilda of Cologne) receiving a beating with rods. Then she can be seen collapsing under the blows by the tomb as a monk reads to her. In the bottom right picture she prostrates herself, healed, at the tomb on which a cowled priest is placing a candle.

neighbourhood of Bury St Edmunds lost a small silver coin at Sudbury. 'A pilgrim of St Thomas has lost his silver coin!' he exclaimed aloud. Three days later at Rochester he put his hand into the purse and found the same silver piece. Ralph, a priest returning from Canterbury, found a spur he had lost some twenty-six miles away on the south side of the river. 'Halves!' cried his companion as he saw the glint of silver in Ralph's hand. The astute priest replied that there could be no halving when a man finds his own property. At the time of the loss, we are told, Ralph had 'deposited a slight and friendly remonstrance in the Martyr's ear'.

A cure performed at a distance required convincing evidence before it found its way into Benedict's ledger of miracles. Beatrice of Woodstock, who had not seen with one eye for four years and the other for seven, found the former healed upon her arrival through the gates of Canterbury and the latter restored after a night in the city. She found Benedict on duty at the shrine and told him her story. Benedict, who noted her mean appearance, tells us: 'I confess my incredulity, if incredulity is a fair name for hesitation felt not on my own account but for others.' Beatrice would not endure a cross-examination and at last 'gave me bad words, calling me hardhearted, wicked, and unbelieving, unfit and unworthy to attend at the tomb of such a martyr, inasmuch as I envied his glory and detracted from his miracles in my excessive anxiety to track out the truth'. At least, however, her determination won her a place in Benedict's book and in history.

Thus the bright springtime of 1171 saw the spontaneous bursting forth of the healing miracles of St Thomas of Canterbury which would spread their ripples far and wide and down many centuries. Before many months elapsed reports of miracles wrought by St Thomas reached Canterbury from as far afield as Germany, France, Italy and Holland, and even on the eve of the Reformation the sick still drank the medicine of the Martyr. As one Canterbury pilgrim's badge declared in Latin, 'For good people who are sick Thomas is the best of physicians.' A carriage-driver of Canterbury had complained in those months that St Thomas took heavy tolls from his trade, for 'I bring him a whole carriage-load of sick folk and carry back only two of them.' For more than three hundred and fifty years every English spring saw the roads to Canterbury thronged with pilgrims on foot or horseback, in litters or carriages. Those roads and trackways today still bear signs of the pilgrims, and to some extent we can follow in their hopeful footsteps, tracing the way from London along the Roman Watling Street, from the west through Winchester, from Farnham along the 'Pilgrims' Way', and finally with them entering Holy Canterbury.

WATLING STREET: LONDON TO CANTERBURY

We owe our most vivid glimpse of pilgrimage to Canterbury in the late fourteenth century to the author of *The Canterbury Tales*, Geoffrey Chaucer. How far he painted the pilgrims from life – thirty-one of them, later joined by a canon and his servant – we shall never know, but in all probability he drew upon his direct observations of individuals. Chaucer himself probably made the pilgrimage to Canterbury, and he may well have met then the originals of the pardoner, the clerk of Oxenford, the miller, the reeve, the knight, the cook, the yeoman, that worldly wife of Bath named Alison, Harry Bailey and all the others.

Pilgrims from the Midlands, the North and East Anglia, as well as Londoners themselves, would have to pass over London Bridge beneath the mouldering heads of traitors impaled on pikes over its gateways. When the first stone bridge was built in 1176 a chapel dedicated to St Thomas Becket stood in the middle, placing the bridge under the protection of the newly popular saint of London. At either end of it, like sentries, stood two churches of Danish saints – St Magnus (see p. 186) and St Olave or Olaf (see p. 70). Before crossing the bridge, however, many pilgrims would have worshipped at the chapel of St Thomas of Acre marking the birthplace of Becket, where Mercers' Hall stands today. (Some think that Becket was called Thomas of Acre because according to one legend his mother had been of Saracen birth, but he probably owed the name to his early adoption by the crusaders. The gilded crescent in the vault of the Trinity Chapel at Canterbury, above his shrine, may be an offering from some returning crusader who had stolen it from a Saracen mosque.)

Once in Southwark there were many hostelries offering bed and board to the travellers who could afford them. Just as some captains in Venice offered all-inclusive 'package tours' to pilgrims heading for the Holy Land, so enterprising hosts like Harry Bailey of the Tabard may have advertised a similar kind of arrangement for the three- or four-day excursion to Canterbury, providing horses if need be as well as lodgings and food, and even a conducted tour.

The two large monastic houses in the low-lying marshes south of the Thames – the Cluniac abbey of St Saviour at Bermondsey and St Mary Overy ('on the island') hard by the ferry – both gave hospitality to pilgrims. Indeed Bermondsey Abbey possessed a Holy Rood which had been fished up in the Thames and worked such wonders that pilgrims flocked to it. 'Go visit the Rood of Northdoor [in St Paul's: see p. 74] and St Saviour in Bermondsey while you abide in London,' wrote John Paston from Norwich in 1465 to his mother, 'and let my sister Margery go with you to pray to them that she may have a good husband before she come home again.' The church of St Mary Overy, much renovated, is now Southwark Cathedral. In the street leading towards Kent stood a hospital called the Loke which housed lazars, those poor people afflicted with such diseases as leprosy who took their name from Lazarus.

When the great fire of 1213 destroyed Southwark the monks of Bermondsey rebuilt their hospital for the sick and poor, many of them pilgrims, on the causeway leading from the bridge called Long Southwark. The hospital of St Mary Overy united with it and the new foundation was dedicated to St Thomas. At first it was a community for poor men and women, a school and an infirmary, all enjoying an endowment from the Bishop of Winchester who had a palace in the vicinity. In 1428 the hospital established its independence from Bermondsey Abbey, and long before then it had given itself wholly to the care of the sick, impotent and lame. The great London hospital of St Thomas is the modern descendant of this early pilgrim hospice called after St Thomas Becket. After the Reformation the authorities called it first 'Becket Spital' and then the Hospital of St Thomas the Apostle. Rebuilt and eventually moved to a different site (opposite the Houses of Parliament), it survives as a monument to the great impulse given to the development of medicine by the pilgrimage to Canterbury.

There were plenty of other great stone houses which would offer food and a place in their rush-strewn halls to pilgrims, for Southwark contained the London palaces of the Bishops of Winchester and Rochester, the Abbots of Hyde (near Winchester), Battle and St Augustine's at Canterbury, and the Prior of Lewes. Their unsavoury neighbours included the occupants of the eighteen stew-houses or public brothels, each with a painted sign along the river bank, whose existence was governed by regulations laid down by Parliament in the reign of Henry II. Next to them rose the walls of the Clink prison for those who proved troublesome in street, hostel, or stew-house. With other gaols, bakehouses and breweries, the borough of Southwark was slowly spreading along the river banks and into the marshes throughout the Middle Ages.

Many pilgrims, particularly those from the poorer classes, would still walk the road to Canterbury in the traditional garb of a pilgrim: woollen shirt belted at the waist, boots tied with thongs, a broad hat, a soft leather scrip (haversack) and a waterbottle, and carrying a stout staff. But others, especially if they were not penitents, chose to ride on horses at least as far as the outskirts of the city. Chaucer's fellowship were mounted, and probably spent three or four days on the fifty-four-mile journey. At what speed did they go? The word 'canter' seems to have derived from the name Canterbury, but it is unlikely that the pilgrims broke into this easy pace until they neared their journey's end. On their bridles jingled rows of tiny 'Canterbury Bells', possibly as a charm to ward off evil spirits. The bridle of Chaucer's monk could be heard jingling 'as loud as doth the chapel-bell'. (These Canterbury Bells gave their name to an English flower not unlike a foxglove which the pilgrims would have seen growing by the wayside.) For the rest of the time the horses walked, with possibly occasional trots to defeat a monotony not always relieved by tales and songs or the playing of musical instruments.

Not far from Southwark Chaucer's miller began to play upon his bagpipes. In the reign of Henry IV an accused Lollard could tell his questioner, Archbishop Arundel of Canterbury:

> I know well that when divers men and women will go after their own wills, and finding out a pilgrimage, they will order to have with them both men and women that can sing wanton songs; and some other pilgrims will have with them bagpipes, so that every town they came through, what with the noise of their singing and the sound of their piping, and with the jangling of their Canterbury Bells, and with the barking out of dogs after them, that they make more noise than if the king came that way, with all his clarions and minstrels. And if these men and women be a month in their pilgrimage, many of them shall be half a year after great janglers, tale-tellers and liars.

The Archbishop replied:

> Pilgrims have with them singers and also pipers, that when one of them which goes barefoot strikes his toe upon a stone, and makes it to bleed, it is well done that he and his fellows begin then a song, or else take out of his bosom a bagpipe, to drive away with such mirth the hurt of his fellow. For with such solace the travail and weariness of pilgrims is lightly and merrily brought forth.

Chaucer mentions the passage of his pilgrims through Deptford, Greenwich, Rochester and Sittingbourne. In other words they followed Watling Street, the main Roman road to Canterbury. Owing to modern road building and urban sprawl there is not much left to remind us of the sights and sounds they

Above: *Charity setting food before pilgrims at an inn. (From Lydgate's translation of Deguileville's* Pélerinage de la vie humaine, *early fifteenth century. British Library, London, Cotton MS Tiberius X.A.vii)*

Below left: *wayfarers at an inn in the late fifteenth century. The bush hanging from the inn sign denotes it as an ale-house. The travellers are seen climbing into the common beds. (From Antoine de la Sale,* Les cent nouvelles. *Glasgow University Library, Hunter MS 252)*

The miller with his bagpipes, from the Ellesmere manuscript of Chaucer's Canterbury Tales, *fifteenth century. (Henry E. Huntington Library and Art Gallery, San Marino, California)*

Rochester Cathedral as it appears from the Norman castle.

would have encountered as they travelled through the apple orchards and cherry gardens of Kent, and paused for beer at the 'ale-stakes', which earned their name from the long poles outside them. Many pilgrims would spend their first night at Dartford. Next morning they forded the River Darent and perhaps prayed in the chapel dedicated to St Edmund on the brow of the next hill, a shrine which attracted so many pilgrims in its own right that the road hither from London was known as 'St Edmund's Way'.

The Templars owned the 'New Work' or 'Newark' in Strood, a pilgrim hospital originally founded by a bishop of Rochester. Certainly before their horses clattered over the wooden bridge spanning the Medway (supplemented by a stone one at the end of the fourteenth century) the pilgrims would have glimpsed the massive Norman keep dominating the walled city of Rochester. The Norman cathedral and monastery church of St Andrew, begun soon after 1080, took many decades to build. None of the buildings where the monks dispensed hospitality to footsore poor pilgrims survives, though the Norman entrance to the chapter-house is still impressive. The north-eastern transept of the cathedral once contained the popular shrine of a pilgrim saint, the Scots baker St William of Perth. This pious man, who gave every tenth loaf he baked to the poor, stayed in the monastery on the night of 20 May 1201 on his way to the Holy Land and was stabbed to death just outside the town when he resumed his journey.

The fate of St William serves to remind us that originally pilgrims travelled in bands not for merry fellowship or cheap party rates but for safety. Before setting out from their parish churches many twelfth-century pilgrims heard this intercession: 'O Lord, heavenly Father, let the angels watch over thy servants that they may reach their destination in safety . . . that no enemy may attack them on the road, nor evil overcome them. Protect them from the perils of fast rivers, thieves, or wild beasts.' Although threatened with most severe penalties, robbers frequently lay in wait for pilgrims. Innkeepers and villagers also often found the stream of pilgrims too much of a temptation. While not as dangerous as the journey to Jerusalem or Compostela, the road to Canterbury possessed its hazards.

Most pilgrims would spend their second night in or near Rochester. By 1316 an inn called the Crown stood on the site of its namesake today; by 1450 the Bull and the King's Head had also made their appearance. Until such luxuries as bedsteads and nightclothes appeared in the fifteenth century, the pilgrims slept on couches, benches or on the floor in beds which consisted of wide long sacks stuffed with hay, straw or rushes. One medieval traveller recorded in his accounts, 'Paid for our bed there (and it was well worth it, witness, a featherbed) one penny.' The poorer pilgrims on foot, who rested at such houses as the Hospital of St Bartholomew at Chatham, would not have much more than some hay or rushes on a stone floor.

Probably at Rochester the mounted pilgrims changed horses, for a well-established system of hiring horses existed on this busy thoroughfare. A horse from Southwark to Rochester cost twelvepence, and the same amount had to be paid between Rochester and Canterbury, compared with sixpence from Dover to Canterbury. These horses bore prominent brands on their flanks to discourage their riders from making off with them.

Eight miles beyond Rochester the road passed through the village of Newington. In the middle of it a cross marked the spot where St Thomas had confirmed some children shortly before his death, not sitting on horseback as most bishops performed the rite but dismounting and placing his hands on the children's heads. In 1171 Benedict, the custodian of Thomas's shrine at Canterbury, had recorded some fourteen miraculous cures among pilgrims at or near Newington. For example, Robert of Essex, blind for ten years and bound for Canterbury, suffered a hurt ankle a mile beyond Rochester when another blind man on a horse – also heading that way – rode over him. Robert lay prostrate in the dust and appealed to the Lord in the name of the Martyr. A few seconds later he found that he could see a stone on the roadway before his face. Jubilant, he ran seven miles to Newington and then onwards to Canterbury.

Five miles beyond Sittingbourne, where Henry V refreshed himself at the Red Lion on his way home from Agincourt and where Chaucer's pilgrims evidently halted, lay Ospringe with its celebrated Maison Dieu, which gave hospitality to all the wayfarers. The buildings stood on each side of the road, and may have been joined by a covered passage. Opposite the surviving part of the Maison Dieu in Water Lane the lower stone courses of the other side can still be seen in the walls of the Crown Inn. Here Henry II reserved a room. In 1360 King John of France gave the master and brothers of the house a handsome present in return for the hospitality he received, as well as alms to four *maladeries* or leper hospices, and also the princely gift of twenty nobles to Sir Richard Lexden, a hermit at Sittingbourne.

In the adjacent town of Faversham the pilgrims could see a piece of the True Cross at the famous Cluniac abbey, which contained the bones of the founder, King Stephen, his wife Matilda and son Eustace. The monks of St Augustine's Abbey at Canterbury held the parish church of Faversham under their patronage. In medieval times pilgrims could worship there in a chapel dedicated to St Thomas Becket.

Now the pilgrims following the undulating Roman road drew near to the hills of the forest of Blean. Before their long ascent Chaucer's company were joined 'at Boughton under Blee' – the village at the western foot of the high ground – by the canon's servant, who was said to be such a powerful alchemist

> That all the ground on which we be riding,
> Till that we come to Canterbury town,
> He could all clean turn upside down,
> And pave it all of silver and gold.

After Boughton Street, as it is now called, the road passes through Upper Harbledown and falls into a valley before the long climb towards 'a little town' called 'Bob-up-and-down', as Chaucer called Harbledown. There they came to the lazar-house of St Nicholas, founded by Archbishop Lanfranc in 1084, where Henry II had dismounted before walking into Canterbury. The Norman chapel, which still survives, has a floor which slopes down to the west door, allegedly to allow it to be washed down after the lepers had walked on it. Edward the Black Prince is said to have drunk from the well here when conducting King John of France prisoner to London. Here too pilgrims would be invited or allowed to kiss a portion of Becket's leather shoe encased in brass and crystal (see p. 71) and to drop their pennies in an almsbox chained to a tree near the gate or fastened to the end of a long pole held out by a leper. This ancient box, with its chain, survives in the almshouses that replaced the old hospital.

Harbledown. The old almsbox once held out to Erasmus is shown here in front of the west end of the church of St Nicholas's Hospital.

Near this village the host in Chaucer's *Canterbury Tales* noted the cook straggling behind and nodding with sleep in his saddle:

> 'Awake, thou Cook,' quoth he, 'God give thee sorrow!
> What aileth thee to sleep by the morrow?
> Hast thou had fleas all night, or art thou drunk?'

As several men slept naked together in the long sackcloth beds stuffed with hay, it is quite possible that fleas from his bed-fellows had kept the cook scratching all night, an experience many of Chaucer's readers would have shared (see p. 156).

On the eastern brow of the hill the pilgrims at last gazed with wonder on Canterbury, the walled city dominated by the cathedral (see p. 66). Erasmus, the great Dutch scholar, who stood there about 1514 with his friend Dean John Colet of St Paul's, described in his *Colloquies* how the cathedral 'raises itself to heaven with such majesty that even from a distance it strikes religious awe into the beholders . . . There are two vast towers, that seem to salute the visitor from afar, and make the surrounding country far and wide resound with the wonderful booming of their brazen bells.'

From this lofty stance the pilgrims hurried down the high-banked road to Canterbury, crossed the River Stour and entered through the West Gate half a mile beyond St Dunstan's Church. Of the six gates which once pierced the city wall only the West Gate has survived the besieging forces of time. Once beyond its portals the pilgrims found themselves in St Peter's Street, amid the noise and bustle of the city.

BY WAY OF WINCHESTER

As the fame of St Thomas spread, pilgrims from Europe began to arrive in large numbers. Merchant carracks and galleys from Venice and Genoa landed them at the Cinque Ports, Portsmouth or Southampton. To meet their needs monastic houses or pious individuals founded *hospitia* in these southern ports. At Sandwich, for example, the poor brothers of the Hospital of St John, founded in 1280, who were allowed to beg on the quaysides, lived in almshouses backed by a hall called the 'Harbinge' where pilgrims could sleep for a night or two. At Dover they would find the similar Maison Dieu, founded in 1227. The beautiful Early English chapel of the pilgrims' hospital at Portsmouth, established by Peter de Rupibus in Henry III's reign, is used today as a garrison church.

Pilgrims from the eastern parts of Europe customarily disembarked at Sandwich. Only two accounts of their travels survive: Wendeck's narrative of the visit of the Emperor Sigismund in 1417 and the Bohemian ambassador's account in 1446. In the Channel they suffered from sea-sickness and 'lay on the deck as if they were dead'. The white cliffs of Dover seemed 'like mountains of snow', while Dover Castle looked 'the strongest fortress in Christendom'. In the crowded port of Sandwich they commented upon the agility of the sailors running up and down the rigging of the ships at anchor. Near Canterbury they were impressed by the great leaden roof of the cathedral, so unlike the tiled churches of their homelands.

Pilgrims arriving at Dover or Sandwich would make straight for Canterbury, but those who came to Portsmouth might well visit the shrine of St Richard at Chichester Cathedral before following the Roman road called Stane Street up to Dorking and then turning eastwards. The Pope canonized Bishop Richard de la Wych in 1260, seven years after his death. Such crowds thronged to Chichester that his body had to be dismembered, so that three stations could be made at the original tomb, a new shrine and a reliquary containing the skull. On 3 April – St Richard's Day – in 1478 the expected crowds were so great that the Bishop banned the carrying of staves, for the pilgrims sometimes used them on each other's heads as they pressed about the cathedral.

Normans, Bretons and others from the southern parts of France as well as Italy and Spain would probably disembark at Southampton, and make their way towards Winchester by the Roman road, a distance of some twelve miles. The Norman chapel dedicated to St Julian the Hospitaller, which belonged to the hostel at Southampton where many pilgrims spent their first night on English soil, still survives as the French Protestant Church.

Beside the water meadows on the southern outskirts of Winchester some of them might refresh themselves at the Hospital of St Cross, although it was not a pilgrim house by design. Bishop Henry of Blois had founded it in 1136 'for the poor of Christ', and made provision for a small college – which survives to this day – of a Master and 'thirteen poor men, feeble and so reduced in strength that they can hardly, or with much difficulty, support themselves without another's aid'. The dress of the thirteen brethren, derived from the Knights Hospitaller, was a long black gown with a silver cross on the left breast: they wear it to this day. Some scores of poor men of the city came daily to eat in the 'Hundred-Mennes Hall'. As it resembles the halls in many pilgrim hospitals up and down the country which have not survived it merits inspection. Pilgrims would have been allowed to spend the night here, lying around the raised hearth in the centre and under the eye of the Master who could watch proceedings through a window high in the eastern wall. The black leather jacks, wood and iron candlesticks, salt cellars and pewter dishes were bought in about 1446, probably from the funds supplied to the hospital by Cardinal Beaufort. To him also are attributed the tall chimneys above the houses of the brethren; like Carthusians they each have two rooms, a pantry and a garden.

The remains of an altar to St Thomas can still be seen in the south transept of the church of St Cross. Like the pilgrims the traveller today can still call at the porter's hatch under the gateway and claim his free 'Wayfarer's Dole': a horn of beer and a slice of loaf. Even more remarkable, he will sup his beer from the same mugs they used, for one of them was fashioned from a horse's hoof in 1326, while the other was made from a cow's horn in the fifteenth century. Nowhere else in England can we drink from the same cups the pilgrims used as they paused on the long road to Canterbury.

From St Cross the pilgrims walked to Winchester Cathedral, which held the famous shrine of St Swithun. The Normans began building the present cathedral for the Benedictine abbey in 1079. By the end of the Middle Ages it looked as it does today – with a total length from east to west of 556 feet, the longest cathedral in Europe. It stands on the site of a much older abbey church in the capital of the Saxon kings of England. Bishop Swithun, the companion and tutor of Alfred the Great, could sternly oppose the boy's elder brother, King Ethelbald, when he broke the Church's laws by marrying his stepmother, but he was not remembered primarily for such actions. A humble and good man, he took to travelling to parishes by night to avoid being cheered by the people, and when he lay dying, in 862, he asked to be buried in the common graveyard under 'the feet of passers-by and rain from the eaves'. Nine years later, according to tradition, the monks of Winchester planned to move him inside the cathedral, but they were prevented by a downpour of rain which lasted forty days and nights – hence his association with the English weather, and the popular belief that rain on St Swithun's Day (15 July) betokens a wet forty days.

The shrine, which at one time stood on a raised platform behind the high altar, became renowned for its miraculous cures and pilgrims from all over England crowded into the inns and hospices of the city. The Benedictine monks of St Swithun's built a hostel for them south-west of the cathedral, known as Strangers' Hall. Fragments of it survive in a house, No. 10 The Close. In the late Middle Ages John Devenish endowed a foundation called the Hospital of St John,

The Hospital of St Cross, Winchester. Above: *the 'Hundred-Mennes Hall', showing the gallery and base of the hammer-beam roof, and some of the Hospital's collection of old pewter vessels.* Below: *medieval drinking cups fashioned from a hoof (left) and a horn. In the background are some of the brethren's houses with their prominent chimneys.*

in the High Street, 'for the sole relief of sick and lame soldiers, poor pilgrims, and necessitated wayfaring men, to have their lodging and diet gratis there, for one night or longer, as their inability to travel might require'.

Into Winchester came pilgrims bound for Canterbury from the West Country. They would have stopped already at Shaftesbury in Dorset to see and touch the shrine of St Edward the Martyr in the abbey church. Any king who met a violent end stood a good chance of being acclaimed a martyr and saint. Edward succeeded to the English throne in 975, at the age of thirteen, and was treacherously murdered in Corfe Castle three years later. Strange miracles at his hastily dug grave beside the road to Wareham led Dunstan, Archbishop of Canterbury, to send men to dig it up. Later the body, said to be incorrupt – a sure sign of holiness – was escorted to Shaftesbury. 'Men murdered him,' comments the *Anglo-Saxon Chronicle*, 'but God glorified him. He was in life an earthly king; he is now after death a heavenly saint . . . Those who would not before bow down to his living body, now bend humbly on their knees in front of his lifeless bones.'

Other pilgrims from the West Country may well have followed a different road through Dorset and visited the large church of St Candida and Holy Cross at Whitchurch Canonicorum in the heart of Marshwood Vale, near the coast between Lyme Regis and Bridport. This parish church is unique in Britain in possessing the relics of its patron saint – St Candida, or Wita – in a thirteenth-century shrine, still the object of pilgrimage. The altar-like tomb is pierced by three oval holes so that the kneeling pilgrim could thrust his head through and make contact with the reliquary. Some eighty years ago a crack appeared in the stonework, allowing the leaden reliquary inside to be examined. It bore the inscription: HIC REQUESCT RELIQE SCE WITE. Within lay the bones of a small woman, thought to be about forty years old when she died. Local tradition says that she was a Saxon woman killed by the Danes on one of the occasions when they landed at Charmouth. (The Viking axe and long-ship carved on the late fourteenth-century church tower are evidence today of the legend.) Nothing more about her is known, though there is a holy well named after her at Morecombelake, a mile to the south, which yields clear cool waters said to heal eye-troubles. Dorset children still call the light blue starry flowers of the wild evergreen periwinkle 'St Candida's Eyes'.

Salisbury Cathedral in Wiltshire could show pilgrims nothing to excite their devotion or curiosity until the canonization of St Osmund in 1456 and the erection of his shrine that year, although the great spire – 404 feet high – built in the first part of the fourteenth century must have served them as a landmark. The old George Inn in Salisbury's High Street was once a medieval hostelry. It was enlarged in the fifteenth century to cater for the pilgrims who came to visit the shrine of St Osmund. Having passed through the carved wooden gateway (which can still be seen), they would have unsaddled their horses in the spacious yard.

The pilgrims rode or walked along the Roman road from Salisbury to Winchester, a distance of over twenty miles, and there they joined the crowds around the cathedral and saw the wonders of the ancient capital. From the stalls down narrow streets and in the markets they bought their provisions – bread, cheese, and hard-boiled eggs – for the next reach of their journey. This would take them north-eastwards to Farnham, in Surrey, thus avoiding the wild forests and bad roads of Sussex. They may have rested at the old Saxon church of St Swithun at Headbourne Worthy, where a great rood of the crucified Christ and his companions above the doorway at the west end would inspire their prayers. Their way would then certainly pass through Alresford. A king of Wessex had given the manor to the prior and monks of St Swithun, and a bishop of Winchester built a palace there which must have provided food for many a pilgrim. In the twelfth century Bishop de Lucy built a canal to connect the Alre with the Itchen so that boats could come up from Southampton. The large pond he constructed to feed the canal with water can still be seen.

Many pilgrims would find shelter at Waverley Abbey, some three miles south-east of Farnham. The oldest Cistercian house in England, founded in 1128, Waverley had seventy monks and one hundred and twenty lay brothers when Thomas Becket was martyred. A large concourse of a thousand abbots, knights, lords and ladies sat down to the dedication feast in 1278 of the rebuilt and much enlarged monastery. The ruins of Waverley stand among green meadows in a bend of the river, retaining an atmosphere of complete peace and tranquillity.

Those pilgrims who supped or stayed in the abbey's guest-chambers may have crossed the River Wey just south at Tilford or even at Elstead, where the five stone arches of the bridge still spanning the river date from the late fourteenth century. It is said that the monks of Waverley were responsible for building six bridges in all over the Wey between Tilford and Guildford. They are unique among surviving medieval examples in that their downstream cut-waters are semicircular. On their way to Farnham, some pilgrims might have paused to see the remarkable wall-painting of the murder of Becket in Bramley Church, fourteen miles north-west of Farnham, which has survived to this day.

The canal reservoir at Alresford, originally much larger.

Opposite: *the modern shrine of St Swithun in Winchester Cathedral, placed in 1962 on the site of his original shrine in the thirteenth-century retrochoir, flanked by chantry chapels of Cardinal Beaufort and Bishop Waynflete. We are looking west, towards the back of the high altar reredos. In the later Middle Ages the shrine also stood on a platform above the row of arches, where coffers containing the bones of St Dunstan and of King Canute and his wife Emma are still displayed. On the floor are medieval tiles, much worn, but a rare survival.*

Above: *St Candida's shrine, in the north transept of the church of Whitchurch Canonicorum, Dorset. Visitors still leave prayer requests and coins within the three openings of the thirteenth-century structure.*

The martyrdom of Becket, a wallpainting of c. *1200 in Bramley Church, Hampshire.*

THE 'PILGRIMS' WAY' FROM FARNHAM TO CANTERBURY

At Farnham, a small town nestling under a castle owned by the Bishop of Winchester, pilgrims from Winchester would be joined by others from the West. Eastwards from Farnham the parties of pilgrims walked or rode along several ancient trackways. The official 'Pilgrims' Way', as shown on Ordnance Survey maps, rests upon comparatively recent attempts – notably by Hilaire Belloc – to link up certain stretches of trackway or lane which are associated with the pilgrims in local tradition. These attempts are mainly guesswork, and there is no clear evidence that one continuous road used by pilgrims ever existed. Even so we can reconstruct their probable route from Farnham to Canterbury, and it is still convenient to call this general line of march from town to town the Pilgrims' Way.

The road from Farnham to Guildford follows the spine of the Hog's Back, a long high ridge of chalk rising to more than five hundred feet, from where the pilgrims could gaze over many miles of countryside to the north and south. A sick or weary pilgrim may have found succour at the church of Wanborough, one of the smallest in Surrey, which stands on the northern hillside. Once six monks from Waverley Abbey celebrated Mass here, and kept the large tithe-barn full of produce from the neighbouring farms and glebe land. But many more pilgrims would have turned southwards to the pre-Conquest church of St Nicholas in Compton, on the southern slopes of the hill, which probably sheltered a relic. For inside the eleventh-century chancel the Normans built a low thick-ribbed vault with a chamber over it. The lower recess held the altar, but the upper chapel, which is screened by the oldest wooden balustrade in England, probably served as a shrine for a noted relic. As a piece of architecture it is unique in Europe. Near the church stand the remains of an anchorite's cell built after the Norman Conquest. The anchorite or hermit could look through a small window at the altar, and ascend to the upper room of the sanctuary. The wooden window board, worn and darkened by the elbows of the recluse, is still there. On the face of the arch near the pulpit some pilgrim or medieval wayfarer has carved a Norman knight in close-fitting helmet beside an eight-armed cross: such graffiti were common in the Middle Ages, and occasionally pilgrims to the Holy Land carried special tools so they could incise their coats-of-arms, crosses or names in the Holy Sepulchre Church. The Norman east window at Compton contains a small image of the Virgin and Child, one of the oldest pieces of stained glass in England.

A knight, scratched in stone to the right of the chancel arch in Compton Church.

At Guildford, taverns or the *hospitium* of the Black Friars at the Dominican friary founded by Queen Eleanor would have provided hospitality for the pilgrims. Apart from some thirteenth-century stone-vaulted cellars under the Angel and a similar vault on the opposite side of the road – possibly once the crypt of the Carmelite White Friars, who erected a cross with a flying angel in the street at that point in 1345 – there are no remains of these buildings. Incidentally, in medieval times the Angel was probably called the Salutation of the Virgin, but after the Reformation the figure of Mary would have been painted over on the inn-sign leaving only the Angel announcing his message. The pilgrims would have seen the Saxon tower of St Mary's Church, midway between the royal castle and the river. Inside we can still see the wall-paintings in the chapel of St John: Christ in glory arrayed in a mantle of imperial purple at his Second Coming surrounded by six other scenes, four representing various episodes – Biblical and apocryphal – in the lives of St John the Baptist and St John the Evangelist. There is also a vivid picture of demons taking away condemned souls, tied up in bundles like firewood, to the fires of hell.

Many travellers on the Pilgrims' Way did not enter Guildford but followed the still visible track to the south of it, which leads from Puttenham to a crossing of the River Wey by a ford near St Catherine's Chapel at Shalford. Built in the early fourteenth century on a knoll overlooking the river, this little chapel – now a ruin – once possessed no less than five doorways, suggesting a storeyed structure inside not unlike the chancel of St Nicholas's at Compton. Possibly it also contained a relic which wayfarers pressed inside to touch.

Having waded across the river with their wallets held high the pilgrims climbed up to the Norman church of St Martha-on-the-Hill, some five hundred feet above the village of Chilworth. 'St Martha' may be a corruption of 'St Martyrs', for tradition relates that six hundred Christians were put to the sword on this hill in Saxon times. The presence of Iron Age earthworks on its southern slopes suggests a former use of the hill as a fort. In 1463 Bishop Waynflete of Winchester granted an indulgence of forty days to 'all those who came for devotion, prayer, pilgrimage or offering to the Chapel; and should there recite the Paternoster, Angel's Salutation and Apostles' Creed, or should contribute towards the maintenance, repair or rebuilding of the same'. Still to be seen are the pilgrims' crosses incised into a stone of the old nave doorway. Some historians believe that the double cross among them shows that a pilgrim returned along the same route.

Bronze Madonna and Child in the church at Shere, believed to have come from a pilgrims' cross.

The North Downs now stretched before the pilgrims. Large crowds of them journeyed eastwards in wintry December in order to keep the vigil of the Saint's day in Canterbury Cathedral, so they would be grateful for the high trackway on the chalk hills which avoided the bogs and muddy roads of the lower ground. Chaucer mentions the 'mire' and 'slough' on the roads of his day more than once. In 1499 a glover from Leighton Buzzard in Bedfordshire travelling to Aylesbury fell into a water-filled hole that a miller had carelessly dug in the middle of a main road near that town in his search for clay to repair his mill. The glover drowned, but the miller successfully pleaded 'not guilty' as he lacked malicious intent.

The main track of the Pilgrims' Way may have led from Albury by way of Shere towards Dorking and Reigate, skirting the steep of Box Hill, thick in those days with box and juniper, oak, beech and whitebeam. At Shere Church the pilgrims scratched crosses and dials on the Norman stonework of the south door. In the north wall of the chancel there is a fourteenth-century quatrefoil window and squint hole, all that remains of the cell occupied by a famous anchoress called Christine, daughter of William the Carpenter. In the middle of the main street of old Reigate there was a chapel dedicated to St Thomas of Canterbury, whose bones lay only another three or four days' journey away. Today the eighteenth-century town hall stands on the site.

Those coming from the Midlands may well have used the pass through the hills north-east of Reigate to join the Pilgrims' Way near Merstham. At the time of Domesday Book the manor of Merstham belonged to the monks of Canterbury. The church once housed a magnificent set of wall-paintings showing the life and death of Becket, but they were destroyed in the last century.

That fate miraculously (as the pilgrims would swear) escaped an even greater treasure in Chaldon Church, two miles to the north. On the oldest wall of the church a Norman artist, at about the time of Becket's murder, painted a scene seventeen feet long and eleven feet high depicting the Ladder of Salvation, leading to hell or heaven. This remarkable picture in red, white and yellow gives us such a vivid insight into the interior world of the pilgrims' minds, and why they undertook a long and tedious journey to seek the aid of holy saints in their struggle upwards on that ladder, that it is worth pausing to look at it as carefully as doubtless they did.

A late twelfth-century wallpainting in Chaldon Church depicting the Ladder of Salvation.

The vertical ladder and the horizontal cloud separating heaven and hell divide the mural into four parts, like a coat-of-arms. In the lower right quarter stands the tree of the Garden of Eden, with the serpent in the branches, which witnessed Adam's fall – the beginning of all human sin. Next to it the wages of sin are displayed. Across hell, men believed, there stretched a bridge as narrow and as sharp as the edge of a saw. It is represented here as a bridge of spikes held up over the flames by two giant demons. Cheating traders are gingerly picking their way across it. Pilgrims would recognize among them the bad blacksmith who, according to popular legend, was condemned to cross the fiery bridge while at the same time fashioning a horseshoe without an anvil. He holds a hammer in his raised hand and is about to strike a horseshoe, already made red-hot by the heat of hell, which he clasps in pincers with the other hand. The man with the bowl is engaged upon a similar impossible ordeal. His yellow bowl contains a white liquid, and he probably stands for all those farmers who had sold short measures of milk. Beneath him, already in the flames, sits the usurer with a fat purse of money hanging from his neck and three bags of gold at his waist. He has no eyes, for usurers could not weep, and two demons leap about him prodding his head with their pitchforks to make him eat more red-hot coins.

In the other quarter of hell a great cauldron of doomed souls is sizzling on hot flames, its inmates stirred up by two monster devils. (An example of such a cauldron as the artist imagined can be seen in Frensham Church, five miles south of Farnham: more than four hundred years old, it measures nine feet round the bowl and stands on a tripod.) The devil on the left suspends with his other hand a cluster of unfortunates who are having their feet gnawed by a demon wolf, indicating that they had used them not for such pious acts as making a pilgrimage but for wanton dancing. A lady who may have given choice morsels of food to her lapdogs rather than to the poor and needy is having her hand bitten to pieces by a hound of hell. Clinging frantically to the lower rungs of the ladder, or toppling off it altogether, are other souls desperately striving to avoid the fork of a devil intent on ruthlessly impaling them before they can climb through the narrow gap in the clouds that leads to the safety of heaven.

Once in heaven the souls mount higher with easy steps and graceful movements, helped by two angels, towards the clouds of everlasting bliss. In the right-hand quarter, the descent of Christ into hell shows the Saviour thrusting the staff of his lance into the mouth of a bound Satan, while Adam, Eve and the souls of the patriarchs fly free. On the left of the ladder the Archangel Michael is busy weighing souls in his scales while a recording angel writes down the measurements. Satan, his tongue slavering like a thirsty hound, has already roped together some souls who are too light in virtue, and he shows all his cunning by trying to press down the scales on his side and win another victim. Above them one happy soul is being air-lifted upwards by an angel in flight. The pilgrims were seeking such help from their saints. For that certain passage they would readily endure the long and tedious tramp through the chalk downs of Surrey or all the way to Jerusalem.

In the fourteenth-century parish church of Buckland, just before Reigate, the pilgrims may have seen the stained glass windows containing the figures of Peter with his keys and a curly-haired bearded Paul holding his sword. But their road lay onwards, passing north of Nutfield, where men dug for fuller's earth as they do today, and Bletchingley with its castle and Norman church. The White Hart Inn, which provided pilgrims with rooms, is said to have been in existence by 1388.

Like Bletchingley, the old town of Oxted would have provided beds and meals for pilgrims who put up at such inns as the Crown and Old Bell. The church stands in a circular churchyard, which may mean that it was built on the site of a pagan stone circle. Beyond Limpsfield the pilgrims at last entered Kent. The Pilgrims' Way on the Ordnance Survey map goes via Titsey Park through Chevening, now the home of the Prince of Wales, and on to Otford. It is a very pretty road which offers easy walking.

Otford Palace, once a manor belonging to the Archbishop of Canterbury, served later as a royal house. Henry VIII and a vast retinue stayed there in 1520 before journeying on to Canterbury and Dover, and thence to a rendezvous with the French King at the Field of the Cloth of Gold. At Otford, according to a detractor in late Tudor times, Becket performed a somewhat spiteful miracle: 'Busy at his prayers in the garden, he was much disturbed by the sweet note and melody of a nightingale that sang in a bush beside him; and in the might of his holiness commanded all birds of this kind to be henceforth silent.' Becket is said to have created the holy spring east of the palace and church by striking the ground with his crozier. Recent research, however, suggests that it was in use in Roman times. Pilgrims joyfully immersed themselves in the waters of Becket's Well, believing they had curative powers. The well now stands in private grounds, where it feeds a large pond.

At Kemsing the wayfarers might well visit the Norman church, which contains a stained glass window of the Virgin Mary made about 1220: she wears a green skirt and a yellow underskirt. In the churchyard there once stood a shrine and statue of St Edith, who was born at Kemsing in 961. A modern window in the church tells her story. Local farmers and yeomen brought grain here to be blessed by the parish priest before mixing it with their seed corn. St Edith's Well can still be seen in the parish.

At Wrotham there are pilgrim crosses cut in the stonework of an open way under the church tower. Possibly the church, dedicated to St George, owned some precious relic because there is a passage (called today the Nuns' Gallery) which spans the width of the church above the chancel arch and is reached by an extension of the rood stairs to the top of the fourteenth-century screen. It might have been used by the guardians of the relic as a watching-chamber, for they could look both east and west through windows. Doubtless they would ensure that pilgrims made their offering in silver coin to the Saint.

After Wrotham some pilgrims would cross the River Medway at Snodland and turn south-eastwards towards Boxley, but others would continue to St Mary's Abbey at West Malling before fording or bridging the river at Aylesford. Not much of the Benedictine foundation for nuns remains today save a ruined tower close to another built as a keep for the fortified manor house. According to legend, when the knights fled from Canterbury after the murder they made their first stop at St Mary's Abbey. They rang the gatehouse bell and asked the nun for food and drink. When they were offered, however, an invisible hand dashed plates and cup to the ground; the knights fled in terror, leaving the nun in dazed confusion. Next day the tidings of Becket's death explained the miracle to the astonished community. Attached to the present gatehouse is a small chapel dedicated to St Thomas, and the guest-house in the grounds still opens its doors to pilgrims or those seeking sanctuary. Not far from the abbey on the road of the medieval pilgrims lay the thirteenth-century castle of Leybourne. The Leybourne family grew wealthy on the wine trade and Sir Roger founded a village called Libourne near Bordeaux. Later he made a pilgrimage to the Holy Land where he died. The small tomb encasing his heart, which was sent home to Kent, can be seen in the church.

The medieval bridge at Aylesford felt the tread of many pilgrims over its narrow humped back. They could find sustenance nearby at the door of the Carmelites or White Friars, for the mother-house of that order had been built here by St Simon Stock and a group of hermits brought back from Mount Carmel in the Holy Land by a crusader, Lord Richard de Grey. In modern times the White Friars have refounded the house and brought back from Bordeaux the skull of St Simon Stock and interred it in a new shrine. They have also restored the ancient guest-house, the Pilgrims' Hall.

Other travellers would break their journey in the hospices and inns of Maidstone, three miles to the south-east, which stood at the junction of several roads and tracks. Here in 1261 Archbishop Boniface built a hospital on the banks of the river for pilgrims

The modern reliquary of St Simon Stock at Aylesford Priory, designed by Adam Kossowski and erected in 1951 to house the skull of the Saint.

bound for Canterbury, of which the chapel (rededicated as the church of SS. Peter and Paul) yet stands. In All Saints' Church a wall-painting also survives showing the presentation of Thomas Becket to St Mary, the original patron saint of the church. Possibly after 1281 some gentle-born pilgrims would sleep in the rebuilt Allington Castle, which stands in a loop of the Medway between Aylesford and Maidstone – that is if they were fortunate enough to know Stephen of Penchester or his descendants.

Near to Kit's Coty House, the remains of a megalithic tomb which testifies to the ancient date of the 'Way', pilgrims coming from Snodland could look out over the Weald set with shining streams, wooded hills and green valleys before they hastened down the winding lanes to Boxley Abbey. Here two remarkable and wonderful sights awaited them: the image of the child St Rumbold and the still more celebrated crucifix from which the Cistercian house derived its name – the Holy Rood of Grace. Tradition related that this sacred object had arrived one day at the monastery on the back of a stray packhorse.

The figure of Christ on the cross concealed a clockwork mechanism and a mesh of wires which enabled the face to assume different expressions, the eyes to roll and weep, the mouth to move, the hands to lift in blessing and the head to bow in sorrow. It was an extraordinary visual aid for men and women who longed to see the living Christ. Like other statues, for example a Kentish figure burnt at Smithfield in 1538 which bowed to receive the prayers of pilgrims, the Boxley Rood belonged to a growing category of such unauthorized popular images. But bishops, despite some disgust, in general looked the other way, and even on occasion defended them against the iconoclastic criticisms of the Lollards. Archbishop Warham could inform Cardinal Wolsey on the eve of the Reformation that Boxley was 'so holy a place where so many miracles are showed'.

St Rumbold, the son of a Northumbrian king, died when he was three days old but not before reciting the Paternoster and Apostles' Creed, a feat which led to him being declared a saint. The small statue of St Rumbold at Boxley could be moved by a child or else prove so heavy that a strong man tugged in vain. In particular girls or women who had lost their chastity could not budge it, and thereby disqualified themselves from kneeling before the Holy Rood of Grace. Those doubtful of their state would make their confession for a fee and then give a generous offering to the attendant priest who – according to later Protestant writers – merely slipped a wooden retaining pin out of a hidden supporting pillar. 'Thus

Kit's Coty House.

Relief of St Thomas Becket, c. *1200, from the façade of the now demolished steward's house at Godmersham.*

it moved more laughter than devotion,' declared the early seventeenth-century divine Thomas Fuller, 'and many chaste virgins and wives went away with blushing faces. . . . '

The ruins of the twelfth-century abbey include part of the refectory and some stones of the gateway that led into the fifteen-acre site. But it is the enormous surviving tithe-barn which testifies to the former wealth of the place. At the Dissolution the agents of Thomas Cromwell could press no more serious charge against the Abbot and nine monks than spending too much of their rents upon wallflowers and roses in the large gardens. However they did exhibit the Boxley Rood in the marketplace at Maidstone, showing to all and sundry the 'certain engines of old wire with old rotten sticks' by which the monks animated it.

Twelve miles down the road from Boxley, passing a castle in Thurnam and a small priory at Hollingbourne, the pilgrims came to the manor of Charing, which King Ethelbert of Kent had given to St Augustine early in the seventh century. Becket would certainly have stayed in the manor-house here, which in later times expanded into a palace. Some of it survives as part of a farm. A broad arched gateway leads into the old courtyard, and there is also a great barn which may have been the banqueting hall of the palace. The parish church at the end of the street once housed a famous relic: the block on which the head of John the Baptist was severed. Richard Coeur de Lion was thought to have brought this relic from the Holy Land and given it to the Archbishop of Canterbury.

After Charing there were sixteen more miles to Canterbury and the pilgrims turned north-eastwards towards the line of the River Stour. In the south chancel wall of Godmersham Church, not far from their path, is an early carved bas-relief of Thomas

Life-size brass marking the tomb of Sir Robert de Septvans in Chartham Church. The seven winnowing fans (used for drying corn) shown on his surcoat and shield are a heraldic pun on his name.

Compton Church, looking from the nave towards the unique upper chapel above the chancel (see p. 55).

Becket, sitting in his vestments and mitre. The Norman castle keep at Chilham heralded the impending end of their journey.

(You may wish to make a slight detour southwards to the village of Chartham to see the brass of Sir Robert de Septvans, the constable of Rochester Castle, who died in 1306. He lies in a full suit of mail under his surcoat, shield and sword at his side. With his mail coif thrown back, his face appears framed in curling hair.)

From Chilham the pilgrims walked or rode along the north bank of the Stour and approached Canterbury through thick woods by an ancient deep road which still scars the side of the hill not far from Harbledown. Alternatively, after Charing they may have turned more northwards and come by Hatch Green and Bigberry Wood towards the same deep way which almost concided with the last half-mile of the Roman road from London, entering Canterbury at St Dunstan's Church.

Opposite: *St Martha's-on-the-Hill, looking from the 'Pilgrims' Way'* *(see p. 56)**. Though high above the village, it is the parish church of Chilworth.*

The Tillingbourne. One path among the ancient trackways kept to the low ground and followed this stream between Albury and Shere.

Above: *the remains of the Bishop's Palace at Charing, one of three archiepiscopal palaces of the See of Canterbury. This structure, now used as a barn, probably served as the great hall. King Henry VIII stayed here on his way to the Field of the Cloth of Gold in 1520.*

Opposite: *Colley Hill, looking west from Reigate Hill. Box Hill lies hidden beyond. During the wet months, pilgrims followed the crest of the North Downs; in summer, they might choose a road through the rich countryside below.*

The tithe barn of Boxley Abbey (see p. 60). Built about 1280, the 186-foot-long building is still in use.

Plan of Canterbury from A Description of England, *1588. The cathedral is in the centre at the top. In front of the gate to its precincts is the market place (numbered 2). Outside the walls to the east is St Augustine's Abbey. To the west, on the inner bridge (near 12), is the Hospital of St Thomas the Martyr. Beyond the West Gate (6) is Harbledown – squeezed on to the map by placing it too far north. (British Library, London, Sloane MS 2596)*

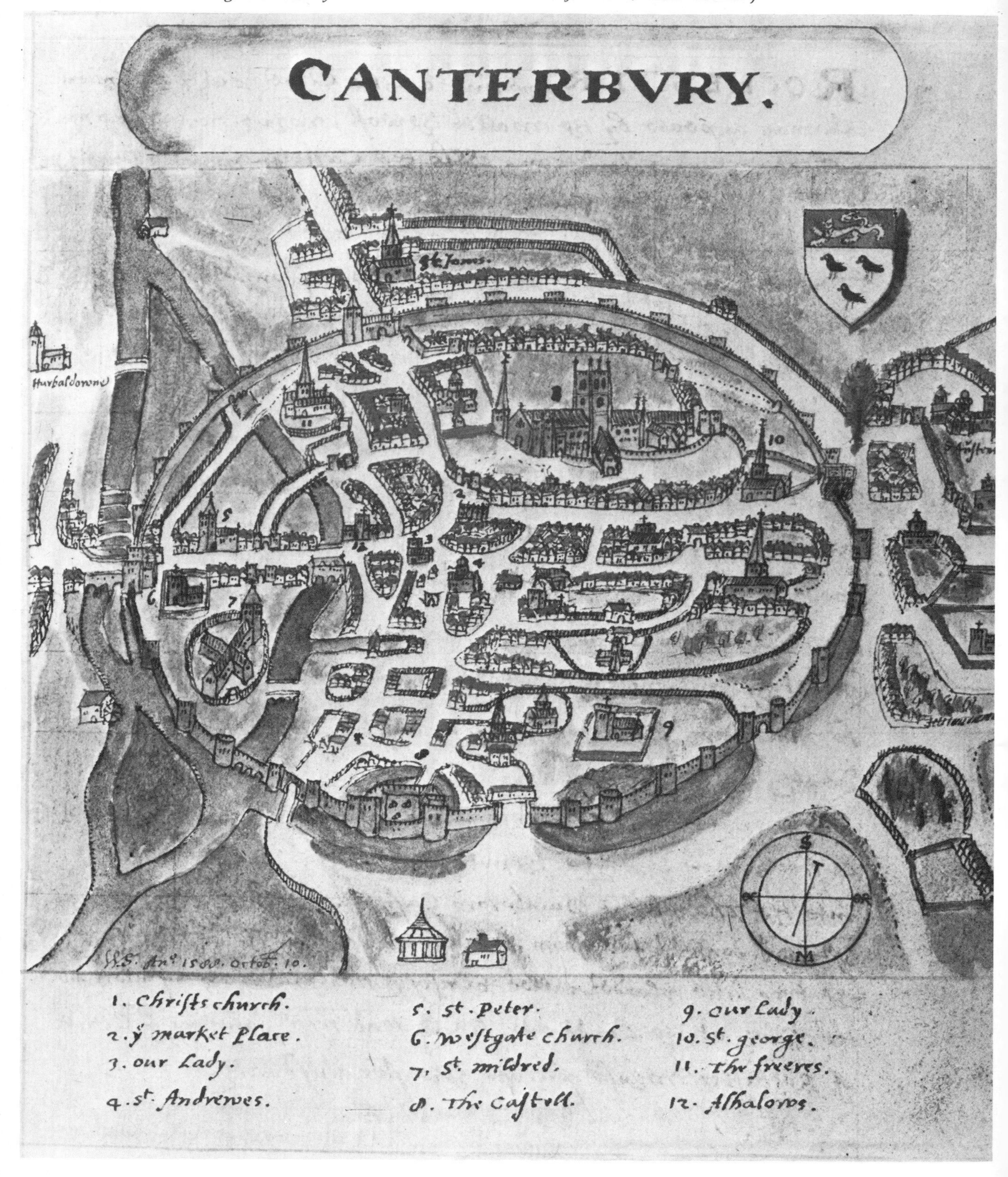

HOLY CANTERBURY

Once inside the walls of the city, its narrow crowded streets overhung by jutting tenements, the pilgrims dispersed to find beds. Doubtless many of them ran the gauntlet of hirelings importuning them to patronize particular hostelries, although city laws at least prohibited innkeepers from running out into the road and physically dragging the weary travellers inside. The Benedictine abbey of Christ Church, with the cathedral as its church and the archbishop as its titular abbot, readily welcomed the poorer pilgrims. The fine Norman staircase, built between 1151 and 1167, leading to the great guest hall in the precincts still stands. Here the statutes of Archbishop Winchelsea laid down that poor pilgrims should be fed daily with fragments of bread and meat, and – like all other social ranks – should enjoy the privilege of being buried in the precincts should they die. St Augustine had founded a second monastery; it lay outside the walls and had served – it will be recalled – as a base for Becket's murderers. Now ruined, it once housed the silver shrine of St Augustine, the Roman apostle to the English, which few pilgrims would leave Canterbury without seeing.

Besides these two monasteries there were plenty of other guest-houses. The Hospital of St Thomas the Martyr at King's Bridge was founded by Archbishop Hubert Walter some thirty years after Becket's death for the maintenance of poor pilgrims and other infirm persons. Archbishop Stratford revised the statutes in 1342 to ensure that poor pilgrims in good health should be entertained only for one night. The eastern branch of the Stour, which runs beside and in part beneath it, doubtless acted as the main sewer. The hospital is now a home for old people, but the Norman crypt and the hall above, similar to that of St Cross at Winchester, can still be visited. To the south are the remains of the Franciscan house of the Greyfriars and the Poor Priests' Hospital, where priests such as Chaucer's parson would have stayed. The Dominicans lived north of the main street, also by the river, and their refectory has survived. There are no remains of the house of the White Friars.

The Chequers, the best-known hostelry in Canterbury, stood at the corner of a lane of stalls selling badges, brooches and bottles, called the Mercery, which was lined on each side with two storeys of shops in arcades, like the 'Rows' in Chester. This led from the main street to one of the cathedral gates. The author of an epilogue to *The Canterbury Tales*, who wrote not long after Chaucer, tells us that the pilgrims arrived at 'mid-morrow' (about eleven a.m.) and lodged at 'The Chequer of the Hope'. After dinner and a visit to the shrine the knight and his son toured the battlements, the wife of Bath and the prioress walked in the garden, and the pardoner waited until the candle was out before he took to the streets in search of illicit love. Only a vaulted cellar which held the casks of wine from which they all drank still survives beneath the later Tudor building.

If they arrived well before dusk the pilgrims probably would have hastened to the cathedral for their first sight of the shrine, hurrying down the Mercery. In the crowds outside the cathedral doors, amid the shouts of street traders, there would be daily scenes of fervent devotion as pilgrims fell to their knees and crossed themselves, prayed, wept or sang and laughed. On the Feast of the Translation (7 July) the annual Canterbury Fair opened its stalls and booths, cashing in on the multitudes of visitors to the city. Long after the cessation of the pilgrimage it continued under the name of Becket Fair.

Inside the cathedral, the monks who acted as guides led the eager visitors to the first of the pilgrimage stations. In the north transept, the Transept of the Martyrdom, they saw the spot where St Thomas had fallen. The column in the centre of the transept against which Becket once leaned was removed to allow a better view. On the Altar of the Sword's Point, erected as a focus for their prayers, they could see two splinters of steel from Richard le Bret's sword which had shattered after his violent blow struck the stonework. (Many artists quite erroneously portrayed Becket kneeling at this altar when the Norman knights slew him.) Inserted into the flagstones a square piece marked the place where the bloodstained pavement had been removed for transport to Rome. In the time of Chaucer's pilgrims, about 1400, the transepts and nave were rebuilt in a soaring Perpendicular Gothic style, but a few courses of the Norman masonry of the wall against which Becket fell remained untouched, and can still be seen today, to the left of the stairs leading down to the crypt, along with a plaque indicating the site of the Altar of the Sword's Point.

Pilgrims who came during the first four years after the Saint's death, like those recorded by the custodian Benedict (see pp. 39–43), would have proceeded from the Martyrdom – many on their knees – up the steps to the high altar, where Becket's body had rested on the night of his murder. Then they descended to the undercroft below the Trinity Chapel, at the eastern end of the Norman crypt. There stood the raised marble tomb of the Saint which is depicted in the stained glass of the cathedral and also in a window at Sens Cathedral in France. Two oval holes in the sides allowed pilgrims to place their heads or hands against the stone coffin (as did the penitent Henry II: p. 38).

In 1174 a disastrous fire destroyed the choir, and for nearly fifty years the stream of pilgrims had to contend with an army of masons, carpenters, plumbers and glaziers – whose wages their offerings helped to pay. The cathedral was enlarged by a spacious raised chapel behind the high altar, built specially for the shrine of St Thomas, its windows filled with glass recording his miracles (see pp. 41, 42). The place was chosen, explained Gervase, a monk at Canterbury under Becket, for its associations with the Archbishop: it stood on the site of the old Trinity Chapel,

> where he celebrated his first mass, where he was wont to prostrate himself with tears and prayers, under whose crypt for so many years he was buried, where God for his merits had performed so many miracles, where poor and rich, kings and princes, had worshipped him, and whence the sound of his praises had gone forth into all lands.

Beyond this new Trinity Chapel or Chapel of St Thomas, at the easternmost end of the cathedral, a unique circular chapel was added to house the *Corona*, 'Becket's Crown', the thin saucer of bone sliced from the Saint's skull.

On 7 July 1220, when the work had been completed in its present form, the young King Henry III and a great assembly of bishops and abbots, lords and ladies, witnessed the translation of St Thomas's bones, borne by Archbishop Stephen Langton up the steps from the crypt. The relics were installed in a gold-plated iron chest that stood on a pink marble arcaded base some six feet high and was covered by a painted wooden lid which could be raised. Seven great candlesticks flanked the shrine like sentries. A net of gold wire like the canopy of a pavilion sagged over the reliquary with an ever growing weight of gifts such as brooches and rings. Indeed during the next three centuries the chapel became a treasure house, as gold cups and a store of sapphires, diamonds, rubies and emeralds accumulated there. Such were the treasures which marked the devotion of Richard Coeur de Lion, of Henry V on his return from Agincourt, of the Emperor Emmanuel from Byzantium and Sigismund the Emperor of the West, of Henry VIII and the Emperor Charles V who knelt there side-by-side in 1520. Here also Edward I had offered the gold crown of conquered Scotland, and Louis VII, who came to pray for his sick child, left behind him the 'Régale de France', a remarkable ruby which glowed on the altar. Twenty-six waggons were needed to cart away those treasures at the Reformation. All vestiges of the shrine itself were removed, but part of the original floor of the 1220 chapel is still there. Around the shrine it was of *opus alexandrinum*, a Roman technique of intricately inlaid coloured marble. In one place the floor is deeply worn by the toes of pilgrims who knelt before the Altar of St Thomas, which stood within an encircling iron grille at the western end of the shrine. (This position, at the 'head' of the buried saint, was usual for shrine altars.) The pavement still shows the stains of the iron railing. In the Corona Chapel, pilgrims would venerate the fragment of Becket's skull, set in a golden and gem-encrusted likeness of his mitred head. The rest of the skull was entombed in the main shrine.

In the cathedral and its rebuilt choir after 1220 the pilgrim could thus visit a number of stations: the Martyrdom, the high altar, the shrine, the head reliquary, and St Mary Undercroft (a famous image of the Virgin that stood on the main altar in the Norman crypt). In 1350, at the time of the Black Death, the offerings of pilgrims at the shrine alone amounted to the great sum of £700. What does seem to have impressed them all, as it does visitors today, is the sense of a long upward ascent to the shrine – many steps up to the choir, more to the high altar, and a final climb to the Trinity Chapel. As one foreign pilgrim wrote, 'church seemed to be piled on church, a new temple entered as soon as the first was ended.'

Throughout the Middle Ages every day saw innumerable common pilgrims swirling and eddying around the cathedral like the tourists of today. On the vigils of the Martyrdom and the Translation they crowded inside the doors to spend the night, the atmosphere warmed by their very numbers and the hundreds of candles burning. Prayers and devotions, secular songs and music, games and even amorous embraces in the shadows enlivened the long night watches. Pickpockets and cutpurses circulated in the packed crowds. At dawn the monks drove them all out in order to prepare the cathedral for the first masses of the Saint's feast. Every fifty years the Translation was commemorated by special celebrations, marked by generous indulgences. The five jubilee years before the last (in 1520) drew crowds of pilgrims from all over Europe.

From the *Customary*, a guide to the duties of the custodians of the shrine written in Latin by two monks – Edmund Kyngston (who died in 1444) and John Vyel – some picture of the daily life in the Trinity Chapel can be formed. The two guardians, one spiritual and the other temporal, slept near the shrine. In summer they rose at five and in winter at six to celebrate Mass in honour of the Martyr, candles burning and incense wafting upwards, assisted by their two lay clerks. Before the fifteen days of the Feast of the Translation they prepared the shrine for the festivities. Every three years they renewed the twelve large candles, which weighed three pounds each and were painted

Two faces of a capital in the crypt of Canterbury Cathedral, showing a griffin and dragon and a lion, carved about 1120.

alternately red and green and set with golden flowers. The barons of Dover maintained another candle wound around a drum, which was equal in length to the circumference of their town. The custodians drew from the cellarer of the abbey supplies of bread, cheese and beer to give to needy pilgrims, though they reserved the right to refresh themselves too from this store.

The *Customary* lists the various expenditures authorized from the coins offered at the shrine. Each day, for example, the custodians paid six shillings and eightpence to the cellarer. At Whitsun and Michaelmas they supplied spices to the monastic community. (Later they gave money instead.) On Maundy Thursday they provided fourpence for each of thirteen poor men after the Prior had washed their hands and feet. Each monk ordained priest received a measure of wine or its value in coin on the day when he celebrated his first Mass at the Martyr's shrine, and each young monk going to Oxford to study got five shillings as pocket money. Every Whitsun the custodians paid forty shillings to the Prior's chaplain for having the hay cut, and at Michaelmas the Sacristan received one hundred shillings for repair work in the shrine's precincts. Every year the custodians bought large quantities of wax for their own altar and the use of the cathedral. Boatmen carried the wax down river from London to Faversham at a cost of a penny a hundredweight, and then carters transported it to Canterbury at double the price.

No pilgrim would leave the precincts without filling his small lead bottle from the Well of St Thomas. Originally it had owed its status to the fact that St Thomas had drunk daily from it, but a legend later than the reign of Edward II attributed the reddish colour of the water to the fact that monks had thrown bloodstained dust into it after the murder. That night and on four others the whole well brimmed with miraculous healing blood, and ever after its water possessed curative powers. Presumably at first the monks issued phials of genuine Water of St Thomas drawn from gallons of well water with one or two drops of dried Martyr's blood in it. A step deeply worn away in the south aisle of the Trinity Chapel is reputed to be the place where pilgrims knelt to receive the 'blood'. As these supplies ran low the monks probably taught that the whole well contained Water of St Thomas. It may have lain on the north side of the choir, but all traces of it have disappeared.

Perhaps on their second or third visits to the cathedral the pilgrims would stand before the other shrines and relics that had brought their forefathers there long before the days of Thomas Becket: those of St Anselm, St Odo, St Dunstan and St Alphege, as well as the head of St Swithun.

Dunstan, Archbishop of Canterbury from 960, loved working with his hands in wood and metal, and thus became the patron saint of jewellers and goldsmiths. He is said to have prepared his own tomb, though his bones were later translated to a shrine on the south side of the choir when the Saxon church was rebuilt.

Of noble birth, Alphege renounced the world in his youth and lived a hermit's life in Bath. After becoming Bishop of Worcester he served as ambassador for Ethelred to the Norsemen after the English defeat at Maldon (991) and converted their leader to the Christian faith. In 1005 he became Archbishop of Canterbury, but six years later the Norsemen returned, burnt down his cathedral and took him

Pewter pilgrim badge of St Thomas Becket, early fourteenth century, found in the Thames at Dowgate and now in the Museum of London. The Saint was noted as a skilled horseman. (The figure of the groom, broken off the large badge, has been made up from another.)

prisoner. Refusing to be ransomed, the Archbishop preached his gospel to his heathen captors and converted some, including perhaps Olaf Haraldsson, who afterwards became St Olaf of Norway. On 19 April 1011 the Danes, angry at his obduracy over the ransom and very drunk after one of their long feasts, hauled Alphege before them, pelted him with ox bones and skulls and finally cut him down with their axes. St Alphege's Church at Greenwich stands on the site of his death. In 1033 King Canute translated the Saint's relics from St Paul's Cathedral to Canterbury 'with great magnificence and bliss and songs of praise' and laid them on the north side of the choir opposite St Dunstan.

After the Norman Conquest Archbishop Stephen Langton questioned the popular veneration of St Alphege, pointing out that he had died not as a martyr for the Christian faith but during the course of a drunken brawl. The theologian Anselm, however, argued that he was a true martyr because he surrendered his life rather than burden Christ's poor with the expense of a ransom. Whether a desire to stamp out Saxon nationalism or to cut down the number of saints in the interests of ecclesiastical tidiness (a process which continues to this day) lay behind Langton's objection we do not know. But these Saxon saints retained their popularity long after the Norman fathers of Canterbury had found a replacement for them in a man of Norman descent slain by Norman swords.

There is no record that Erasmus paused to visit these ancient Saxon saints during his visit with Colet to Canterbury in about 1514. Coming as no ordinary pilgrims, being friends of Archbishop Warham, they saw the same sights as countless pilgrims before them, and more. Erasmus mentions seeing the stone statues of the murderous knights in the south porch. Passing through an iron screen inside the church, he and Colet knelt at the wooden Altar of the Sword's Point and received a piece of le Bret's sword blade in their hands – 'the sacred rust of this iron, in love of the martyr, we religiously kiss.'

Descending to the crypt, they found other priests waiting to show them a silver head reliquary enclosing a skull, the forehead left bare to be kissed. (This was probably a relic of St Dunstan.) Erasmus also saw hanging in the gloom of the crypt the celebrated hair shirt and drawers, girdles and bandages which Becket had used to mortify his flesh – 'horrible even to look at, and a reproach to our softness and delicacy'.

Up in the choir, the monks unlocked various aumbries or cupboards full of ivory, gilt and silver boxes of relics and offered them to be kissed. Colet recoiled with disgust from the reputed arm of St George with dry blood and flesh on it. One Christ Church inventory lists some four hundred holy items, such as a piece of St Cuthbert's beard and two teeth of St Alban, as well as eleven arms, three hands kept in a great ivory chest near the high altar, and the bodies of twelve saints buried there. Doubtless the scholars were shown such treasures as pieces of Our Lord's manger and sepulchre, and part of the column to which the soldiers bound him to be scourged, for they are listed in the Christ Church collection. Here also the two companions saw richly ornamented altar-pictures of St Thomas, possibly on the high altar near the cross, and various articles kept under the altar. In the sacristry in the north aisle (probably the chapel of St Andrew) as a special privilege they were allowed to inspect Becket's silken vestments, candlesticks and pastoral staff – a light cane covered with silver plate about waist-high – and his plain silk pallium and sudary (face cloth) stained with blood. The Saint's crozier may also have stood here. It was originally of pear-wood with a crook of blackthorn, though later generations enriched it with gold and silver.

In the Trinity Chapel, as they gazed on the treasures around the shrine, Colet asked the custodian monk whether it would please St Thomas if the poor took away all those gold and silver coins. When the custodian looked distinctly angry Erasmus put down some pence to mollify him. Then Prior Goldstone opened up the shrine for them. 'A coffin of wood,' wrote Erasmus, 'which covered a coffin of gold, was drawn up by ropes and pulleys, and discovered an

Canterbury Cathedral, seen from the west.

invaluable treasure. Gold was the meanest thing to be seen there: all shone and glittered with the rarest and most precious jewels of an extraordinary bigness; some were larger than the egg of a goose.' The Prior pointed out each offering in turn with a white wand, giving its name (in French, for the benefit of foreigners), its value, and its donor's name.

The two scholars then returned to St Mary Undercroft, where an altar covered with costly offerings stood hedged in by a double iron screen. Finally, in the sacristy the Prior produced a black leather box and all knelt. It contained a fragment of linen marked with dirt, and had apparently been used by Becket 'to wipe the perspiration from his face or his neck, the runnings from his nose, or such other superfluities from which the human frame is not free'. Pursing his lips in a characteristic way when he felt annoyed, Colet declined to accept a piece of it and accepted instead a glass of wine before setting out.

Their road lay 'very hollow and narrow' through high banks up to Harbledown, where the old men of the almshouses ran out, sprinkled them with holy water and offered them the brass-bound leather upper of Becket's shoe to kiss (see p. 47). 'What, do these asses imagine that we must kiss every good man's shoe? Why, by the same rule, they might offer his spittle or his dung to be kissed', retorted Colet, and once again – this time out of pity – Erasmus restored harmony with the gift of a coin.

The vast majority of visitors to Canterbury in the Middle Ages lacked the critical spirit of these two Renaissance scholars. Sprinkled with holy water, penance complete and the benefits of indulgence secured, they left the cathedral for the May sunshine, October rain or December snow in the streets outside. Lead badges depicting the Saint in his bishop's dress on horseback (he was a great horseman), or with his mitred head stamped *Caput Sancti Thomae* (representing the reliquary in the Corona Chapel), would be purchased with other Canterbury badges from the booths and hawkers clamouring for custom. Small bottles of Water could be bought by those who had forgotten to fill their own at the Well of St Thomas. These could all be sewn on to hats or cloaks, and taken home as proof that the pilgrimage had been truly made. Before the pilgrims stretched the long journey back to the familiar world of the village where they would be surrounded by regular miracles of the seasons and sustained by the gift of the Mass, the bread of heaven.

Canterbury Cathedral, looking west across the Trinity Chapel. Becket's shrine stood between the inlaid circles in the foreground and the more elaborate pavement beyond, on this side of the high altar. As the holiest place, it was later flanked by the tombs of the Black Prince (on the left) and Henry IV (right). Note how the floor levels fall to the west.

Opposite: *steps leading up to the Trinity Chapel from the south side, hollowed by the feet of countless visitors. The Black Prince's tomb can be seen at the top. In the Jubilee Year 1420, 100,000 pilgrims are said to have visited the shrine; in 1970, 125,000 came to commemorate the eight hundredth anniversary of St Thomas Becket's martyrdom.*

London *St Erkenwald and St Edward the Confessor*

As befits a capital city, London in the Middle Ages contained not only great churches but also famous relics. Only the base of some chapter-house buttresses remains of Old St Paul's Cathedral, leaving to our imagination the vast length of its Norman nave and Gothic choir (together, nearly six hundred feet), and the lofty steeple, at least fifty feet higher than Salisbury's spire. In a room below the chapter-house the canons used to melt down the candles set up by pilgrims before the celebrated image of Our Lady of St Paul's, regarding even these wax offerings as part of their emoluments. Certainly people thronged the precincts of the cathedral. In 'Paul's Walk' inside the nave horses were bought and sold, servants hired, lawyers met clients and sweethearts embraced. Fairs overflowed from the churchyard into the church, with butchers, tanners and cheese-makers raucously hawking their wares under the Norman arches.

The bones of the celebrated St Erkenwald, an Anglo-Saxon bishop of London, were translated in the fourteenth century to a rich shrine behind the high altar. With its own altar to the west, it stood enclosed within a gilded and painted wrought-iron grille, presented about 1400. At about the same time an English poet wrote a masterpiece of alliterative verse entitled *St Erkenwald*, and it gives us an insight into the beliefs of pilgrims about the power of saints. In it Erkenwald questions an uncorrupted corpse, arrayed as king and judge, which has been discovered in a splendid tomb in the foundations of St Paul's. He asks it to identify itself, and the corpse replies that in this life it was a pagan judge of perfect integrity and therefore buried with royal honours. God, the divine lover of justice, had crowned the praise of men with the miraculous preservation of his body. Erkenwald asks if the same God, who promises heaven to the just, has also saved his soul. No, replies the judge, for he had not known the Christian faith and good deeds are not enough. Weeping with compassion St Erkenwald intercedes for him, praying that the corpse may be vivified long enough for the giving of baptism. As he does so a single tear falls from the Saint's cheek upon the face of the corpse. It sighs and cries out that the baptism of that tear has saved its soul.

The shrine of St Erkenwald in St Paul's Cathedral, recorded in an etching of 1657 by Wenceslaus Hollar. An inscription celebrates the survival of the memory of St Erkenwald through a thousand years, two fires, and the fury of a populace 'in whom faith is extinct'. Only eight years later shrine and cathedral perished in the Great Fire of London.

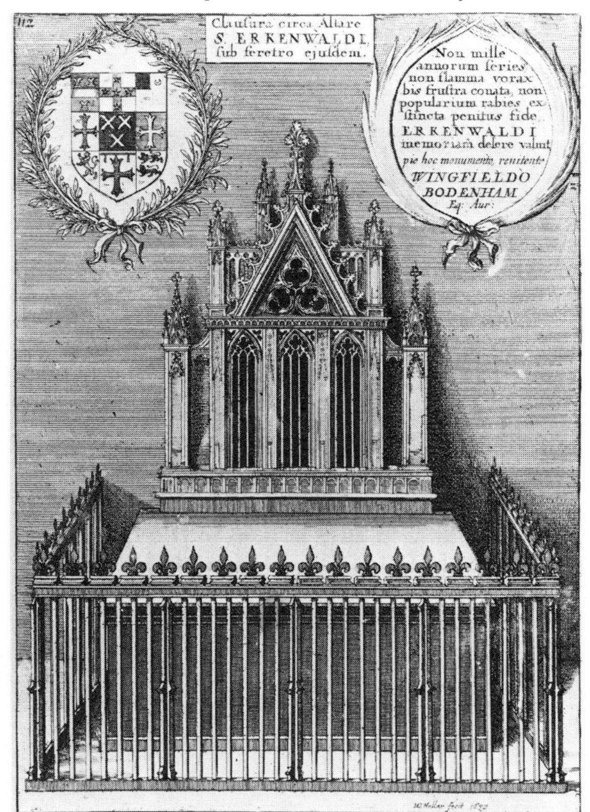

Pilgrims would have no difficulty in identifying themselves with that pagan judge; they also needed help, the assurance of a blameless saint's intercession on their behalf. Hence the popularity of St Erkenwald's shrine. Here, for example, the captive monarch King John of France made an offering of twelve nobles. Richard de Preston, grocer, gave his best blue sapphire stone to remain on the shrine to cure infirmities of the eyes, and Thomas Samkyn, squire to the Abbess of Barking, hung up a silver girdle as a token of his gratitude for some act of intercession.

St Paul's also contained a famous miraculous rood, the *Crux Borealis* or Rood of Northdoor (see p. 44). Said to have been carved by Joseph of Arimathea, it stood on a beam spanning the north transept. It attracted many pilgrims and offerings: in 1368 Thomas Maurice bequeathed his black girdle with silver buckles to the Rood, a blue girdle to the shrine of St Erkenwald, and a yellow one to the image of St Mary in the Lady Chapel.

Other statues of the Virgin Mary in London drew pilgrims, such as a famous image at Willesden. These local pilgrimages must have provided occasions for immorality among the less inhibited Londoners, for one medieval preacher saw fit to warn the citizens against them. 'Friar Donald preached at Paules Crosse that our Ladie was a Virgin, and yet at her pilgrimages there was made many a foule meeting; and loud cried out, "Ye men of London, gang on yourselves with

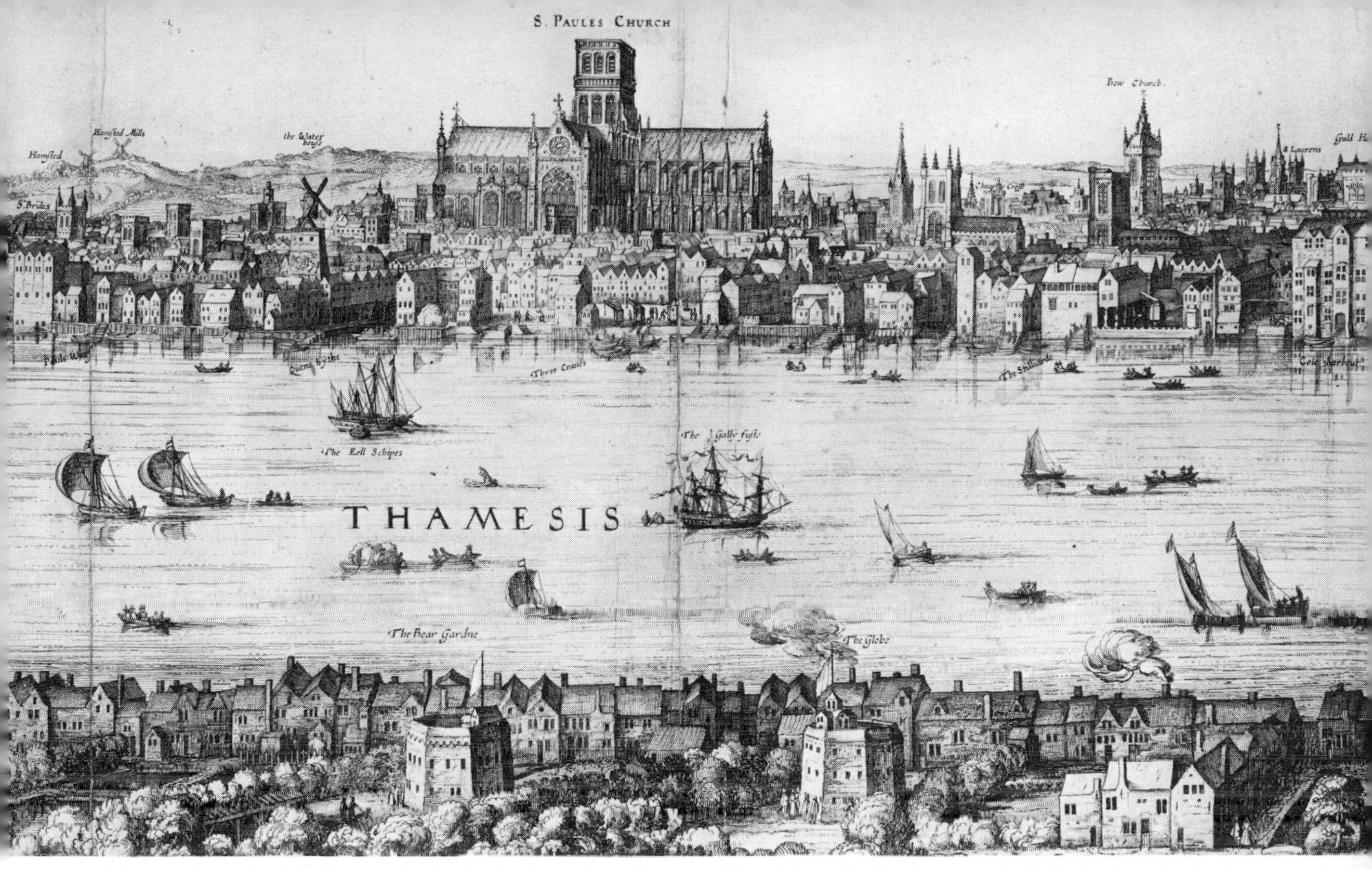

Old St Paul's Cathedral, from J. C. Visscher's View of London . . ., *1616. We are looking from Bankside in Southwark; London Bridge was downriver to the right.*

your wives to Wilsdon, in the divel's name, or else keepe them at home with you, with a sorrow."'

Before the martyrdom of Becket, the citizens of London accorded first place in their devotions to St Edward the Confessor in Westminster Abbey. His shrine remained the special focus of royal devotion: around it are the tombs of eleven kings, queens and princesses, and on the great Coronation Chair nearby monarchs have been crowned for over six hundred years.

The half-French King Edward died on 5 January 1066 and was interred before the high altar in the monastic church he had built. Long before his canonization in 1161 he had been acclaimed as a saint by the people, mainly on account of seven healing miracles and his reputed chastity. William I knelt before his tomb and subsequently rebuilt it to the glory of the Saint. It is not difficult to see a political motive here: a search for spiritual legitimacy by the bastard Norman conqueror. Certainly the Normans needed the Saint's authority and support behind them. According to legend, when William ordered the Saxon St Wulfstan of Worcester to resign his see the Bishop laid his pastoral staff on the tomb of St Edward, who had appointed him. No one could move it and so, it is said, William was compelled to retain Wulfstan and to make a new tomb.

William's younger son Henry I ordered the opening of the tomb in 1102 to verify the rumour that the Saint's body had not seen corruption. Abbot Crispin presided over the ceremony, with Bishop Gundulf of Rochester present as a witness. To their delight they saw the unperished flesh of Edward the Confessor; a gold crown encircled his long white hair, a sceptre lay at his side and a ring upon his finger. The Abbot severely rebuked Gundulf for trying to pull some white tufts of hair from the Saint's beard to take home to Rochester as a relic.

Queen Eleanor, wife of Henry II, often walked barefooted to the Confessor's tomb, and on one occasion she made an offering of some hair from the head of Mary Magdalen. On 13 October 1163 Archbishop Thomas Becket translated the remains into a magnificent shrine built by Henry II. The corpse of St Edward had still not corrupted; his royal robes showed no sign of decay and again eye-witnesses saw the royal insignia and the ring of St John on the pale finger. Thomas and King Henry, assisted by the Abbot of Westminster, lifted the body from the old to the new tomb, with the monks holding up the lid of the feretory. (The word 'feretory', derived from *feretrum*, the bier, means both the chapel in which a saint is venerated and the ceremonial coffin containing his bones, which is set on the pedestal or base of the

Pilgrims at the shrine of St Edward the Confessor in Westminster Abbey, creeping in and out of the apertures which permit them to touch the tomb. From La estoire de Seint Aedward le Rei, c. *1250. (Cambridge University Library, MS Ee.3.59)*

shrine. Where anything of a medieval shrine survives today it is almost always this pedestal, the bones having been cast out and their casing of gold and jewels broken up.) An illustration in the mid-thirteenth-century biography *La estoire de Seint Aedward le Rei* shows the shrine, with a number of pilgrims venerating the relics or praying while two creep through openings in the base, under the watchful eyes of a monk. In the foreground there are what appear to be votive candles, of the sort made to the same length or weight as the suppliant and then coiled round.

After the completion of the choir of the new abbey church, which he was rebuilding at vast expense in the form that we see today, Henry III gave orders for a second translation of the relics to a new shrine between the Lady Chapel at the east end and the high altar, which had been moved westwards almost into the centre of the church to make room for it. Labourers piled up earth said to have been brought from the Holy Land to build a platform for the shrine, so that all could see it. For nearly three centuries Londoners celebrated the anniversary of the Translation, which took place on 13 October 1269. Processions of monks, friars, and nuns from all over London, accompanied by the citizens, their wives and children, walked to Westminster Abbey to leave their candles burning before the Saint's shrine. In 1390 Richard II, who made St Edward his patron saint, attended the great celebrations. His portrait, now in the Sanctuary, the oldest contemporary painting of an English sovereign, may once have hung on the shrine. Twenty-three years later Henry IV was seized with a sudden fatal illness as he prayed at the shrine before setting out for the Holy Land. On 6 July 1483 Richard III walked to the tomb barefooted with his wife.

In time the shrine of St Edward glittered with rich royal gifts. Already in 1236 Henry III had an image of his new queen, Eleanor, placed there, and he added the heart of his nephew Henry in a golden casket. Edward I gave a fragment of the True Cross encrusted with gold and jewels, and also offered the Scottish royal regalia and the 'Stone of Destiny' from Scone Abbey. This ancient stone upon which Scottish kings sat to be crowned is perhaps the only medieval votive offering at a British shrine which can be seen to this day. The Stone of Scone possessed its own mythical

Opposite: *the shrine of St Edward the Confessor. The shrine altar stands at its west end. To the east stood the famous Relics Altar, near the bridge-like chantry chapel of Henry V. On the south is the tomb of Edward III.*

history as a relic. Some medieval people identified this worn block of reddish sandstone as Jacob's pillow at Bethel. Possibly it was the seat or pillow of St Columba in Iona, removed from there to Scone Abbey by King Kenelm II around the year 840. The massive oak Coronation Chair was made in 1300–1301 specially to contain it.

Two further gifts commemorated a story that is also illustrated in the mid-thirteenth-century biography of St Edward. King Edward had given his ruby ring to a man dressed in the habit of a pilgrim who asked him for alms in the name of St John the Evangelist. Later, two English pilgrims, lost in the Holy Land, gratefully accepted the offer of a venerable white-bearded man to lead them to Jerusalem. There he revealed himself as St John, who had tested the devotion of King Edward in the guise of a humble pilgrim, and sent them homewards with the royal ring to return it to the King with the prophecy that they would meet in heaven within six months. Edward II set two gold figures of St Edward and St John as the pilgrim on twisted pillars at the western end of the shrine, and Henry VI incorporated the legend in the stone screen that still stands behind the Coronation Chair. In keeping with this royal custom of munificent gifts Henry VII placed a gold and enamel image of himself in a kneeling position on top of the shrine.

Despite the bruising of time, and without its clothes of rich blue paint and gilding, the seven-foot-high pedestal of the shrine of St Edward stands today in the Chapel of the Confessor. Henry III employed a craftsman who called himself Petrus Romanus, Peter the Roman, assisted by a fellow-Italian Odericus, to make it, as an inscription now barely visible beneath the lower plasterwork records: 'In the year of our Lord 1270, this work was finished by Peter a Roman Citizen. Reader, if you would know how it was done, it was because Henry was the present saint's friend.' The inlay of red and green porphyry and the twisted shafts with remains of gold and white glass mosaic are typical Roman work, and traces also remain of the Roman pavement of marble inlaid in patterns, dated 1268, similar to that of Becket's chapel at Canterbury.

Countless pilgrims have pushed heads or hands under the trefoil arches of the arcades at each side. The stone step worn by their knees can still be seen, although it has been relaid and the hollow is now on the inner edge. The Renaissance canopy, presented by Mary Tudor in 1557 and usually covered by a pall given by Edward VII in 1902, replaced the ancient wooden cover which was destroyed under Henry VIII. Originally painted to resemble malachite, it suffered damage itself when in the days of James II some scaffolding fell and broke open the feretory. A choirman helped himself to the crucifix of pure gold and enamel, on a gold chain two feet long fastened by a locket set with four red stones. What happened to the diadem of gold on the skull, or the pieces of gold, coloured silk and linen that lay among the brown bones, history does not relate. The choirman gave the cross to King James, and later the Young Pretender seems to have presented it to the Pope.

The monks would show pilgrims other precious relics in the aumbries around the shrine: the footprint of Jesus on the rock of the Ascension, which the Dominicans gave Henry III; a crystal phial of the Holy Blood, a gift from the Patriarch of Jerusalem; and the Virgin's Girdle, which English queens borrowed as a talisman against dangerous childbirth. Edward I brought back from France the skull of St Benedict and some clothes worn by St Peter.

To be buried in the same church, let alone the same chapel, as a saint was accounted a great privilege. Not unnaturally many English kings and queens chose to lay their bones close to the powerful relics of St Edward – the Confessor's wife Editha, Henry III, Edward I and Queen Eleanor, Edward III and Queen Philippa, Richard II and Anne of Bohemia, Henry V, and daughters of Edward IV and Henry VII.

From the Conquest onwards St Edward the Confessor served more as the patron saint of English kings than as the guardian of England or even of London. Common pilgrims did not give much money at his altar, nor did many seek his healing miracles. They visited the great shrine, however, if only to gaze upon the rich display of treasures and to feel themselves – like modern tourists in Westminster Abbey – close to the mystery of kingship.

The Stone of Scone, set into the Coronation Chair in Westminster Abbey.

Windsor *John Schorne and Henry VI*

In 1475 Edward IV began the rebuilding of the royal chapel in Windsor Castle, the chapel of the Knights of the Garter. The glory of God and the provision of a fitting burial place for himself served as motives, but doubtless the glory of the House of York also preoccupied his mind. The Tudors, who completed that magnificent canopy of stone fan-vaulting breaking out like foliage, certainly adorned the work with their own devices – their royal monograms, coats-of-arms, the portcullis and English rose badge.

Though the accession of the House of York probably killed the proposal that the Lancastrian Henry VI should be canonized, the memory of this pious, gentle, befuddled and indeed feeble-minded monarch lived on and the veneration of him as a saint developed spontaneously. After his death in the Tower of London from natural (or, some said, violent) causes in 1471, his body was buried in Chertsey Abbey. Stained glass windows, altars and statues commemorated him in many churches; a little chapel which once stood on the medieval stone bridge at Caversham proudly displayed the dagger which had allegedly killed him. Pilgrims made their way in ever larger numbers to the King's lowly tomb. Doubtless after consulting Edward IV, the Dean and Canons of Windsor thought it prudent to secure the relics of a saint who would divert these pilgrims to St George's Chapel instead and draw others for the fame and enrichment of their foundation. Their choice fell upon a Buckinghamshire saint, John Schorne. (They soon had Henry VI as well, as we shall see.)

John Schorne exemplifies the uncanonized popular saints whose cults spread in the later Middle Ages. He had served as rector of North Marston in Buckinghamshire from 1290 until his death in 1314, the year of Bannockburn. He achieved fame as an exorcist and miracle-worker, apparently specializing in cures of the ague and gout. When the owner of a dead ox was faced with ruin Schorne raised it to life, and the well which bears his name he created by striking the ground with his staff during a severe drought. It is said that in a contest with the Devil he compelled his adversary to enter one of his boots. Thus rood-screens at Sudbury in Suffolk and Gateley, Suffield and Cawston in Norfolk show him holding a boot with the Devil in it – a winged and horned dragon of hideous visage according to the Cawston painting. (The existence of these four screen paintings suggests that John Schorne enjoyed much popularity in East Anglia.) His action could be interpreted as conjuring the devil of pain out of a leg. It is said that his power to make the Devil pop in and out of a boot gave rise to the toy known to all children as 'Jack-in-the-Box'.

Pilgrims flocked to Schorne's Well for its healing properties and to his shrine in the parish church, where the south aisle was probably the site of his elaborate tomb. But after 1475 the Dean and Chapter of St George's Chapel successfully supplicated Rome for permission to transfer his relics to Windsor. Having thus obtained this valuable property, doubtless to satisfy their consciences they gave money for the building at North Marston of the superb chancel and two-storeyed vestry and sacristy.

John Schorne conjuring the Devil from his boot. A fifteenth-century painting on panel, formerly in Sudbury Church and now in the Gainsborough House Museum.

Opposite: *the chancel of North Marston Church.*

Meanwhile at Windsor a richly decorated shrine in the south-east chapel had been prepared for the relics, enclosed by an iron grille which can still be seen. In 1585 the Elizabethan Chapter removed Schorne's bones to some unknown spot when they gave permission for the chapel to be transformed into the Lincoln Chantry on the burial of the Earl of Lincoln. But for his brief century before the Reformation the Saint drew pilgrims to Windsor like bees to honey. Bishop Latimer in a sermon referred scathingly to pilgrims 'running hither and thither to Mr John Schorne or to Our Lady of Walsingham'. A fifteenth-century manuscript at Windsor contains what might have been a pilgrim's hymn, beginning 'Hail, gem of pastors, O John, flower of teachers, rector of Marston.' In the list that then follows of his virtues and miracles, he is described as the 'liberator of the weak from toothache', the rescuer of the drowning, and the 'heavenly consoler of wretched boys who are in sadness'. Those 'harassed by the pain of fevers' could in particular turn to him for help. The hymn ends by asking God to 'grant thy mercy to all fevered persons who honour the memory of thy priest, John, that if it be thy will, fevers may have no power to trouble them further.'

But the rival wonder-worker to Master John Schorne had also been lain to rest in St George's Chapel. In August 1484, on the orders of Richard III, the body of Henry VI was moved from Chertsey Abbey to a new burial place in the aisle south of the high altar, under vaulting painted with his badges and emblems. His helmet still hangs above his grave and a fine iron almsbox designed for the shrine by John Tresilian, with an elaborate Gothic letter H, is also preserved. According to the contemporary account of John Rous, an antiquary of Warwick, the disinterred body was 'very odiferous, not indeed from spices employed when it was buried by his enemies and tormentors. And it was in great part incorrupt, everywhere entire as to the beard and hair, with the face as usual, though somewhat sunken, with a more meagre appearance than ordinary.'

Pilgrims came from afar to worship at the tomb of 'Holy King Henry' and offer their coins, candles and wax sculptures. With awe they inspected his relics: his cap (mysteriously transformed into red velvet), which cured any headaches if worn for a while; his spurs; a wooden piece of his bedstead; and two linen sheets from his death-bed.

From the stories of miracles collected and partially investigated as evidence for canonization, we catch some vivid glimpses of the pilgrims. Henry Walter of Guildford, for example, who was wounded by cannon in a seafight and put overboard into a small boat, saw a vision of Henry dressed as a pilgrim, with blue gown and leather scrip. Once on shore he sent his sister to Windsor carrying his own likeness in wax, and when he had recovered sufficiently he came himself. The Abbess of Burnham brought a young boy who had fallen while bird-nesting in April. Stephen Payne and Henry Lugey of Caversham, carters, bore a picture in wax of the help they had received from the Saint: their waggon overturned between Reading and Aylesbury and a cask of wine burst open, but they instantly invoked the Saint who stemmed the flow and miraculously restored the contents. William Bartram of Caunton in Nottinghamshire gave thanks for a healed rupture, caused when one of his opponents at football kicked him and not the ball. Young Miles Freebridge of London, who swallowed a round silver badge of St Thomas of Canterbury, implored the aid of Henry VI and then spat it out. The relatives of John Ashe, whose son had fallen into a half-filled well, came barefooted to Windsor. William Sanderson of Norfolk, bound for London, had run his vessel aground on a sand bank tearing out fifteen rivets; the Saint delivered him, and he brought to Windsor a wax model of the ship as a thanks-offering.

King Henry VII opened the proceedings of canonization for his uncle, and built a magnificent chapel east of the Lady Chapel in Westminster Abbey to house a new tomb. But the long process came to an untimely end during his son's reign and when the chapel with its fan vaulting was eventually completed his own bones were buried there with those of his wife Elizabeth. At Windsor the shrine of Henry VI disappeared during the Reformation, but the coffin came to light again in 1798, lying in a vault, and an inscribed slab marks its position today. Every year on the vigil of 6 December and 21 May scholars of Henry's two foundations of learning lay white lilies for Eton and red roses for King's College, Cambridge, on the grave during evensong, commemorating the birth and death of the royal martyr.

The choir of St George's Chapel in Windsor Castle, hung with the banners of the Knights of the Garter: an early nineteenth-century view, looking west from the high altar. The shrines of John Schorne and Henry VI were in the south choir aisle, beyond the piers on the left.

The West

Glastonbury *'And did those feet . . .'*

Glastonbury Tor is a distinctive hill over four hundred feet high which towers at the western end of a spur in the Mendips. *Torr* is an Old English word for an abrupt or lofty hill. Before modern drainage the Tor rose out of a fresh-water marsh, for in early times the tidal waters of the Bristol Channel, some fifteen miles away, flooded the low-lying land between the Mendips and the Quantock Hills. It formed the highest point of a small island in those flat marshes which stretched for miles thick with willow, alder and hazel and alive with wild fowl of many kinds.

When the West Saxons occupied the area soon after 658 they found a Celtic monastery below the Tor at Glastonbury, established by monks from Wales or Ireland. King Ine of Wessex (688–726) refounded and rebuilt this monastery, granting it lands and privileges. But its history remains obscure until 940 when Dunstan became abbot. Under his aegis the abbey became a spearhead of Benedictine reform in the English Church. Claiming to be the oldest monastery in England, Glastonbury also became one of its larger and more wealthy houses. Indeed one wit said that if the Abbot of Glastonbury married the Abbess of Shaftesbury they would form the richest couple in the realm.

The fame of Glastonbury rested upon a legend, first written down in the twelfth century, that the Christian faith was brought to England by St Joseph of Arimathea in AD 63 or even earlier. According to the story, the Apostle Philip, who had just converted Gaul, sent him with a band of missionaries to carry the good news into the islands of Britain. Joseph brought with him the Holy Grail, the cup used at the Last Supper, which Pontius Pilate had given to him and in which he had caught Christ's blood during the Crucifixion. After many adventures Joseph and his companions made a landfall somewhere in the south-west of England and made their way towards Glastonbury Tor. Exhausted by their journey they rested on a hill about a mile south-west of Glastonbury, a place thereafter known as Weary-all Hill. Reaching the Tor, St Joseph made ready to pray. His hawthorn staff, which he thrust into the soft ground, immediately sprouted with delicate white flowers.

The Abbot's Kitchen seen from the ruined south transept of the abbey church, with the site of King Arthur's black marble tomb in the right foreground. The kitchen was part of the rebuilding of the Abbot's House carried out by Abbot Breynton in the mid-fourteenth century.

St Joseph decided to settle on the firm land near the foot of the Tor, called in Celtic *Ynys Witrin* or the Isle of Glass, and live there as leader of a small community of hermits. Guided by the Angel Gabriel, the companions built the *Vetusta Ecclesia*, the Ancient Church, the first Christian church in Britain. Christ himself is said to have appeared in order to dedicate it. In another version of the legend the young carpenter of Nazareth came to England and made this 'church of boughs' with his own hands from wattle and daub on a timber frame, in honour of his mother the Virgin Mary. Preserved by the monks, the Ancient Church attracted pilgrims from all over England. When fire destroyed the abbey in 1184 a new chapel rose at once on the site of the Ancient Church, and partly on its foundations, at the west end of the great church. The speed of the rebuilding indicates its importance: the chapel was completed in two years, by 1186, the abbey church not until the middle of the next century. The crypt of this Lady Chapel, and subsequently the whole, became known as St Joseph's Chapel (see p. 88), and it survives as an intriguing ruin to this day.

St Joseph was also said to have buried the Holy Grail in an unknown place near Glastonbury Tor, and this became the seed of the other Glastonbury legend – the quest for the Grail by King Arthur's Knights of the Round Table. Glastonbury is thought by many to be the Isle of Avalon, where King Arthur after his last battle was spirited away. In 1191 a Glastonbury monk saw in a vision the coffins of Arthur and Guinevere in the adjacent burial-ground between two pyramids. Thus the abbey acquired another reason for fame. Could Arthur have been buried there? According to Celtic mythology, Avallach, the ruler over the dead, lived in a realm called *Ynys yr Afallon* (the Isle of Apples), somewhere in the western seas. Although there is no written evidence earlier than the twelfth century linking Glastonbury with this Avalon, doubtless a long oral tradition held that Glastonbury Tor once marked the Island of the Dead, a sacred burial place for Celtic chieftains and their families. Thus the first Christian missionaries may deliberately have chosen to build their church on this prominent pagan sanctuary.

Nature abhors a vacuum, and so did the medieval mind in matters as vital as religious history. By the late Middle Ages the monks had completed a somewhat speculative history of Glastonbury from the time of Joseph to the arrival of Dunstan. In this tradition the first Christian settlement reverted to wilderness after the last of Joseph's twelve companions died. In response to a request from a British king in 166 Pope Eleutherius sent two missionaries called Phaganus and Deruvianus to convert his pagan subjects. They found their way to Glastonbury where they came upon the

A fragment of one of the bones of St Paulinus in an early Tudor reliquary, now in Glastonbury Museum.

deserted and ruinous church of St Joseph which they restored. Near it they built the first stone church on the site. After converting the local tribes the two Roman missionary priests died at Glastonbury, where their bones attracted pilgrims as late as the thirteenth century. In the fifth century St Patrick is said to have arrived at the island and organized the hermit monks who worshipped in the two churches into a community with himself as the first head. In later times a Monk of Glastonbury had a vision informing him that St Patrick's body lay buried to the right of the altar, and so his tomb augmented the wonders awaiting the pilgrims to this hallowed place.

St Patrick's name drew other Celtic saints such as St Bridget and St Indract to Glastonbury, or so the chroniclers inform us. Shortly afterwards St David settled there for a time with seven companions, and it was claimed that he lay buried at Glastonbury. There is some real evidence that northern monks brought the relics of St Aidan, the early Bishop of Lindisfarne (see p. 143), and St Paulinus, appointed Bishop of York by St Augustine, to Glastonbury for safekeeping when the Danes ravaged the North. In the town museum today there is a tiny reliquary containing a small piece of bone said to belong to St Paulinus and to have been given to the monastery by St Augustine.

Glastonbury has an importance within the development of the English national identity. In a sense the legend of Joseph's sojourn expressed that English sense of being a special nation, called by God for some high purpose, which flowered again and again in the following centuries. A nation whose origins were intermingled with the people and instruments of Christ's passion, and thus summoned to holiness – such was the deepest feeling in the English spirit, not altogether lost under the secular skies of more modern times. In visiting Glastonbury, its ground seeded with saints and heroes, the pilgrim must have felt that he stood near the very soul of England.

But the legend also illustrates most vividly the need which lay behind pilgrimage: the quest by simple, practical and concrete-minded people to find something to act as a stepping-stone between themselves and the geographically distant and spiritually abstract concepts of the Christian religion. This may well be a true human longing in medieval people which could be expressed in the Arthurian romances as the quest for the Holy Grail. One means of bridging the gap lay in going to the Holy Land to see and touch the places associated with Our Lord. By other – miraculous – means, Joseph of Arimathea and the living blood of Christ came to England. Later generations embellished the story by making Joseph into a wealthy merchant trading in Cornish tin, who sent his 'nephew' Jesus to Cornwall to look after his business. During these years of his early manhood, the 'hidden years' of the Gospel narratives, as mentioned above it was imagined by some chroniclers that Jesus came to Glastonbury and built with his carpenter's tools the *Vetusta Ecclesia* which Joseph subsequently found when he arrived in AD 63. Thus by the exercise of creative imagination, the unfamiliar is made familiar by this transposition of Jesus to these shores: the seeming chasm between first-century Palestine and medieval England is wonderfully spanned. Glastonbury became a Holy Land in miniature, a place certainly hallowed by the mystical body of Christ in the Holy Grail and probably by his fleshy presence in the years before the public ministry in Galilee.

> And did those feet in ancient times
> Walk upon England's mountains green?
> And was the holy lamb of God
> On England's pleasant pastures seen?
> And did the Countenance Divine
> Shine forth upon our clouded hills?
> And was Jerusalem builded here
> Among these dark Satanic mills?

Blake's words capture the wonder and awe of the medieval pilgrim at Glastonbury, eager to believe all that the learned monks could tell him. But even they could not show him the tomb of St Joseph of Arimathea. In June 1345 one John Blome, acting under divine inspiration, obtained from Edward III a licence to search for these precious relics within the bounds of the abbey. A chronicler recorded under the year 1367 that 'the bodies of Joseph of Arimathea and his companions were found at Glastonbury'. Curiously, the monks seem to have refrained from pointing out the burial place – an unusual reticence which suggests a real ignorance. What they could show was the famous Glastonbury Thorn, the rooted staff of St Joseph, which flowered every Christmas in praise of the Nativity.

Miracles worked by St Joseph certainly attracted pilgrims. William of Malmesbury, who knew Glastonbury before the fire of 1184, called its treasure of relics 'the heavenly sanctuary on earth'. The cult in the later Middle Ages centred on an image of the Saint placed in his chapel in 1382 by Abbot Chinnock. No representation of it exists, but it probably showed the Saint holding (as he does in the fifteenth-century stained glass window at Langport Church and on the screen at Plymtree in Devon) two 'cruets', tall stoppered jugs like those used to hold the water and wine at Mass. According to one legend, it was they rather than the chalice that Joseph brought with him, and they are depicted on the Saint's heraldic shield as devised by Richard Bere, Abbot from 1494 to 1524. Bere also built a chapel in memory of King Edgar, whose bones he translated with great ceremony, and parts of it still stand.

The monks of Glastonbury maintained their claim to possess the bones of St Dunstan, a story hotly disputed by Canterbury. After their own fire in 1184 they raised a new shrine to him, alleging that after the Danes burnt Canterbury Cathedral in 1011 a party of monks from Glastonbury journeyed there and found the Saint's bones among the hot embers of the collapsed roof. When they drew near Glastonbury with them the abbey bells rang of their own accord. As pilgrims came in increasing numbers the monks of Christ Church sent to Glastonbury letter after letter of protest. Eventually in 1508 Archbishop Warham opened the tomb in Canterbury, and found in the wooden coffin a case of lead containing the bones and a leaden plate inscribed *Hic requiescit Sanctus Dunstanus Archiepiscopus*. In triumph he wrote to Abbot Bere informing him of this discovery and directing him to abandon all claim for his 'Dunstan' under threat of excommunication. The Glastonbury monks insisted that they possessed the relics, entrusting to one of their number the task of handing down the secret of the burial place to a successor. But the Reformation soon broke this incipient chain of tradition.

Pilgrims who once thronged the church nave could read the history of Glastonbury and its list of indulgences on parchments pasted on the wooden leaves of a frame fastened to a pillar or wall. This late fourteenth-century *Magna Tabula* has survived and is today in the Bodleian Library at Oxford.

The George and Pilgrim Inn in the town is the finest surviving example of a hostel built especially for pilgrims in the Middle Ages. When Abbot Selwood presented it to the Chamberlain of the abbey in 1490 it no doubt looked much as it does today, with its stone mullioned windows, battlements and armorial bearings. Constructed for some reason now obscure, an underground passage once linked the cellars of the inn with the abbot's chambers in the monastery.

Today only substantial ruins remain of Glastonbury Abbey. The richly arcaded Lady Chapel, or Chapel of St Joseph, stands complete to roof level. Stones among the green grass show us the outline of the church, and some of its walls, especially at the transept, survive to an impressive height. The Abbot's Kitchen, square outside and octagonal inside, retains its tall roof and the massive lantern which both lit and aired the room below. Trees said to have descended from the Holy

The George and Pilgrim Inn, Glastonbury.

Thorn, Joseph's staff that had rooted itself, can also be seen in the grounds. They belong to a winter-flowering strain of hawthorn. There is no record that the Chalice Well, an inexhaustible spring on Chalice Hill under Glastonbury Tor, was pointed out as the hiding place of the Holy Grail before the eighteenth century, but it may have been visited as a healing well long before then. On the Tor itself the tower of St Michael, all that remains of a church, stands guard over the past. Before it the agents of Henry VIII hanged, drew and quartered the eighty-year-old Richard Whyting, the last abbot of Glastonbury, and two of his monks; but neither the Reformation nor the secular centuries which followed it have quite dispelled the mysteries that cling to this former island in the marshes.

The Lady Chapel at Glastonbury, known also as St Joseph's Chapel, and the ruins of the great church, looking towards the high altar and the towering ruins of the transepts.

St Joseph with his cruets, portrayed on the fifteenth-century rood screen in Plymtree Church, Devon.

Gloucester *Edward II*, Winchcombe *St Kenelm*, Hailes *the Holy Blood*

The first Christian saints apart from the companions of Christ were the Roman martyrs. Their relics worked miracles. In succeeding generations the association between sudden violent death and sanctity lingered just below the surface of conscious thought, ready to erupt into spontaneous devotion to an uncanonized saint. As already noted, royalty possessed from early times a mystique which increased the chances of such a popular posthumous veneration. But men prominent in public life, names on everyone's tongue, could qualify. A monk of Evesham Abbey, for example, compiled a book of miracles performed by the relics of Simon de Montfort, killed at the battle of Evesham in 1265. Pilgrims found healing powers in the waters of Earl's Well or Martyr's Fountain, a spring in Battlewell Ravine where Montfort had fallen. At his tomb they knelt and applied to their heads a *mensuratus*, a cord which had been used to measure his bones and which also proved to have miraculous properties.

In 1266 Henry III, fearful that these miracles might be interpreted as God's vindication of the Earl's cause, prohibited the pilgrimage to the relics of Simon de Montfort, who, being excommunicate at the time of his death, could never have been canonized anyway. Fifty-eight years later, however, Edward II wrote in a letter that people still venerated Montfort, and flocked to a gibbet in Bristol where the dry bones of some of his followers hung in chains. He complained that bogus miracles were enacted there expressly to render the King odious to the people. The political aspect of pilgrimage became even more plain in the veneration of the implacable enemy of Edward II, his cousin Thomas, Earl of Lancaster. After his beheading at Pontefract in Yorkshire in 1327 the local people renamed the place of execution St Thomas's Hill and built a chapel for the pilgrims who flocked there. Many churches, including St Paul's Cathedral, acquired pictures or statues of the new 'saint' despite the fury of King Edward. At South Newington in Oxfordshire there is a wall-painting showing Thomas of Lancaster kneeling in prayer while the executioner raises his sword for a second blow. In the same church St Thomas of Canterbury is also depicted in a mural, evidence perhaps that the two saints had become linked in popular imagination.

Yet Edward II himself seems to us the strangest candidate for such impromptu canonization. Despite his faults of character and his indulgence of such damaging favourites as Piers Gaveston, he remained surprisingly popular. His subjects did not protest when he was deposed, but they certainly objected to the supposed violent manner of his death. His successors, in league with Queen Isabella, kept him captive first at Kenilworth and then in Berkeley Castle, where they probably murdered him in secret on 21 September 1327 (a scene portrayed on two bosses in the north transept of Bristol Cathedral). This news caused a wave of anger and pity throughout England. Possibly in the face of some competition from the Abbots of Malmesbury, Kingswood and Bristol, the Abbot of St Peter's at Gloucester came and collected the corpse, and interred it at royal expense in the north aisle near the high altar in Gloucester Cathedral. Tradition relates that royal stags drew the bier, hence the representations of them upon the tomb. Among the expenses of the funeral, Thomas of Berkshire received payment for a silver vase used to enclose the heart of Edward II.

Almost immediately miracles at the tomb were reported and pilgrims came there in increasing numbers. The Abbot sought from Rome the canonization of the King, but without success.

Head of the effigy of King Edward II, carved by a master at the court of Edward III, probably about 1340. It is the earliest important sculpture to be made of English alabaster.

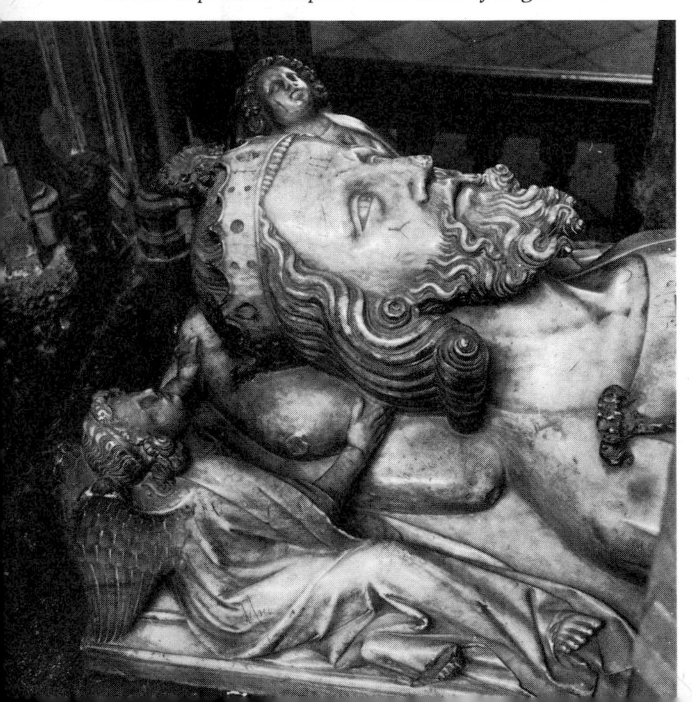

Opposite: *the tomb of Edward II. The effigy of the King, with angels at his head and a lion at his feet, lies below a uniquely ornate canopy of white limestone, on a base of limestone and dark Purbeck marble.*

The gallery and yard of the George Inn at Winchcombe.

Nonetheless the pilgrims continued to come and they saw the beautiful tomb with angels supporting the crowned head of the monarch, which fortunately still awaits the visitor to the cathedral. It stands in a glorious choir rebuilt between 1337 and 1350 by order of the murdered King's son, Edward III, and financed in part by the offerings of pilgrims. The galleried New Inn in Gloucester is said to have been erected as a pilgrim hostel, and the Bell at Tewkesbury makes a similar claim.

In the great abbey of Winchcombe in Gloucestershire lay the bones of another English king who also died as political victim rather than martyr and attracted thousands of pilgrims to his healing shrine. At the age of seven, so tradition says, Kenelm succeeded his father Cenwulf as King of Mercia in 821, but his sister Cwenthryth instructed her lover Ascobert to take the boy hunting for deer in the thickly-wooded Clent Hills and to murder him there. Ascobert carried out the foul deed, and buried the corpse on a remote hillside under a large rock. One day, the legend continues, a white dove flew into the basilica of St Peter's in Rome while the Pope stood before the high altar and dropped at his feet a parchment scroll bearing these words:

> In Clent, In Cowbage, Kenelme Kyngborn,
> Lyeth under a thorn his hede of[f] shorn.

The Pope sent orders to Wulfrid, Archbishop of Canterbury, to investigate this mysterious message. Guided by a white cow, the searchers dispatched by Wulfrid found the shallow grave containing the body and an iron sword. From under the stone a spring of pure clear water appeared. Both rock and well can be seen today. Shortly afterwards, two parties of monks from Gloucester and Winchcombe converged on the scene, and wrangled like holy black crows for the relics. At evening one astute brother (presumably from Winchcombe) suggested that the weary disputants should sleep there that night and whoever awoke first should have the bones. But when the Gloucester monks rubbed their eyes the following dawn they found that their rivals had stolen a march on them. They set out in pursuit. Exhausted by the heat and a sleepless night, with the Gloucester relic-hunters coming into sight, the Abbot of Winchcombe called a halt on Sudeley Hill. Where he struck the ground with his staff water gushed out. Much refreshed, the monks renewed their steps and brought their treasure safely home. Subsequently pilgrims would follow their steps, worshipping at the chapels built later beside each of the two miraculous wells.

The monks buried St Kenelm beside his father at the east end of the abbey church and venerated him as a martyr and saint, although of course he was never formally canonized. Cwenthryth heard the bells ringing for her brother while she was reading the Psalms backwards (a practice in devil worship). The sound of the joyous peals caused her eyes to be torn from their sockets and to fall upon the page. This dire fate is portrayed in carved stone on the west front of Wells Cathedral, where St Kenelm stands over a woman collapsing on an open book. History records the fact that Cwenthryth had become Abbess of Southminster by 824, but it does not tell us whether or not blindness afflicted her.

How true is the story? The *Anglo-Saxon Chronicle* names the successor of King Cenwulf as his brother Ceowulf, and makes no mention of Cenelm or Kenelm. But he certainly existed, for ninth-century charters bear his name. Moreover, in 1815 early archaeologists opened the two stone coffins near the altar of the abbey church. One held the remains of a mature man; the other contained a boy's bones – and a rusted short iron sword. These relics have long since gone, but the coffins can be seen in the fifteenth-century parish church built in the days when Winchcombe prospered in the wool trade.

Nothing substantial remains of the once magnificent abbey of Winchcombe, but a pilgrim inn put up by Abbot Richard Kidderminster in the reign of Henry VII still does business under the sign of the George. The Abbot's initials, 'R.K.', stamp it with its monastic origins. The galleried yard of the inn is an unusual survivor from the early Tudor period: it is not

difficult to imagine pilgrims tightening up the girths of their horses here for the long ride home.

On their way, however, they would almost certainly stop at the Cistercian abbey some two or three miles away in order to see 'the Holy Blood of Hayles'. According to tradition, these drops came from a vase enclosed in a leaden box inscribed *Jesu*

Hailes Abbey. We are looking diagonally across the cloister towards the triple arcade of the chapter-house. Between it and the trees beyond is the site of the abbey church choir, where the Holy Blood was venerated.

Christi Sanguis, which came to light in Mantua in 804, a second phial being unearthed in a hospice garden there in 1048. In 1267 Edmund, son of Richard, Earl of Cornwall and founder of Hailes Abbey, purchased a phial of the relic from the Count of Holland and brought it back to England. He gave one-third of the Holy Blood to Hailes. (The other two-thirds went to an Augustinian house founded shortly afterwards at Ashridge.) The monks at Hailes received the relic with much ceremony. They at once began to rebuild the east end of their church (on the model of Westminster Abbey) to accommodate the shrine, and the Abbot appointed one of them to display the Holy Blood to pilgrims and to receive their gifts.

Aware of the manufacture of false relics, many medieval people approached such wonders as the Holy Blood at Mantua, Rome, Bruges, Fécamp in Normandy and Hailes with some doubt. As the writings of Thomas Aquinas confirm, men could accept relics of the Divine Blood emanating from a eucharistic host or miraculous statue of Christ, but they baulked at blood from the actual wounds of the crucified Lord. Robert Grosseteste, Bishop of Lincoln, answered the doubters in 1247 by arguing that Nicodemus and Joseph of Arimathea would have been splashed with the Holy Blood as they took the body down from the cross, while the disciples might have gathered up the precious essence on the five occasions when Christ shed blood.

At the Dissolution the commissioners appointed for Hailes Abbey, led by Bishop Latimer, declared that the Holy Blood appeared translucent red in a glass phial held in a reliquary of smooth beryl richly worked with silver, 'and after we did take our part of the said substance and matter out of the glass then it was apparent glistening yellow colour, like amber, or base gold, as doth cleave to as gum, or bird-lime.' In November 1539, before consigning the fluid in the phial to the flames at Paul's Cross in London, the Bishop of Rochester pronounced it to be 'no blood, but honey clarified and coloured with saffron'.

The principal remains today of this once-great pilgrimage centre are several arches of the monks' cloister, and, in the site museum, six carved bosses.

A stone roof boss, c. 1270, found in the ruins of the chapter-house at Hailes. It is thought to represent Christ as the spiritual Samson rending the jaws of the lion (the Devil); its size, some two feet across, suggests that it came from the abbey church.

The saints of Cornwall

Cornwall is separated from England by the wooded Tamar valley; it is a sea-girt peninsula thrust out into the Atlantic Ocean. These geographical facts have deeply influenced its religious history. After the withdrawal of the Romans and the invasion of England, except for the western parts, by pagan Saxon tribes, the Christian faith was kept alive in Cornwall by Celtic missionaries, mostly from Ireland but also from Wales and Brittany, who landed in sandy coves and bays among the coastal cliffs. These early Celtic holy men were called saints, but beyond their names little is known about them. They lived as hermits in caves or beehive cells, mortifying the flesh by such practices as chanting the Psalms while standing waist-deep in cold streams. The dedication to Celtic saints of Cornish churches prevents their names from slipping into total obscurity. A few late Celtic crosses still survive. Moreover, many Cornish churches stand on the site of a holy man's cell, often quite far from the village of the parish. As the hermits chose caves or cells near fresh water there is often a holy well or spring near these ancient churches.

St Piran, an Irish missionary who came with his mother and St Ives to bring the gospel to the Cornish, has left us the oratory which he built on the north coast and where he died on 5 March in about the year 480. His converts buried him beneath the altar, and when in the tenth century shifting sands silted up the church they built another a mile hence and removed the Saint's head to it. At the Reformation, however, the head was returned to the skeleton in the earlier chapel. In 1835 antiquaries uncovered fragments of this primitive oratory from the sands once more, and found beneath the altar slab three headless skeletons. Lying between the legs of one of them were the three heads replaced there in the sixteenth century. Since the excavation, however, unscrupulous modern vandals have stolen the lot. Perhaps the relics of St Piran have wrought their own revenge.

In a field beside the church of St Melor at Linkinhorne there stands a holy well in a late medieval structure, one of many that once existed in the county. It is not hard to discern the traces of pagan worship behind this veneration of springs or wells, its origins being in the animistic belief that every tree, mountain and water had its spirit. Even within the Biblical tradition there is mention of wells with healing properties: the pools of Bethesda and Siloam at Jerusalem are but two examples. The traveller on the road to Samaria can still drink water from Jacob's Well. In a famous letter to Abbot Mellitus in 601, Pope Gregory the Great advised Christian missionaries in England not to prohibit recourse to the ancient sanctuaries but to consecrate them in Christ's service, rededicating them with the names of saints and

St Keyne's well. A small granite house protects the spring.

martyrs. thus the early Christians built their churches on holy mounds or even within stone circles, and heathen springs were simply renamed after saints or holy hermits. From time to time Christian kings attempted to stamp out the old pagan religious customs. The Canons of Edgar (963), for example, ordered the 'withdrawal of worship from trees, stones or fountains'. But these ancient heathen beliefs remained visible through the white surplice of Christianity.

The wells of St Cleer and St Keyne near the town of St Germans in east Cornwall are examples which can be seen today, the former famous as a *bowsenning* pool (a Cornish word for immersing oneself in a holy well with healing powers). It was said to cure the insane. St Keyne, the tutelary saint of the other well, is reputed to have been a daughter of Braganus, Prince of Brecknockshire, who flourished around the year 490. Country people believed that a husband or wife drinking first from the waters of her well would gain mastery over the other spouse. As Southey wrote in his ballad 'The Well of St Keyne':

> A well there is in the west countrie
> And a clearer one never was seen,
> There is not a wife in the west countrie
> But has heard of the well of St Keyne.

The church of St Neot is built some three hundred yards from one of the oldest wells in Cornwall. A later well-house has replaced the original arch of stones which once stood over it. Victorian villagers could recall their older relatives bringing weakling children to be washed in its waters. Inside the church some glowing stained glass recounts the story of St Neot and his well amid other scenes drawn from the Bible and figures of Cornish saints. The finest of all Cornish Celtic crosses stands in the churchyard, with four other ancient crosses for company.

Pilgrims also made their way to holy wells for the purpose of divination. The wells at Gulval, Roche and Nantswell in Cornwall were widely renowned for this power. The pilgrims resorted there on the eve of the feast of the saint to whom the well belonged, and spent the night watching or 'waking' there. The person anxious about the future then dropped a small object such as a bent pin or a crooked sixpence into the waters, and paid an old wise man or woman to interpret the bubbles that rose to the surface. At Nantswell the pilgrims walked to the water on Palm Sunday, bearing crosses and an offering to be handed to the attendant priest. Each threw his palm cross into the spring, believing that if it remained on the surface he would outlive the coming year, and if it sank then death awaited him before next Palm Sunday. This practice at Nantswell illustrates two general rules for those visiting all holy wells. First, a particular day and time had to be observed: daybreak or sunrise on May Day or the summer solstice, and later Easter and Ascension tide, were common choices. Secondly, the spirit of the well had to be placated with an offering.

In the Middle Ages a great many pilgrims made their way in great numbers to St Michael's Mount, the chief shrine in Cornwall, to seek the aid of the Archangel Michael. According to an old Cornish legend, in 495 some fishermen saw the Archangel upon a rocky ledge on the western side of the Mount. Because of the imagery of St Michael leading his winged legions against the hosts of hell in the sky, churches upon such high hills or mountains were often dedicated to this prince of angels. Long before 495, however, the Mount served as a hill fort, sea haven and market for traders drawn to Cornwall by the tin mines. It is probable that even before the coming of the Celtic Christian missionaries the heathen Cornish venerated it as a holy hill. The Elizabethan poet Edmund Spenser in his *Shepherd's Calendar* wrote:

> In evil hour thou took in hand
> Thus holy hills to blame
> For sacred unto saints they stand
> And of them have their name
> St Michael's Mount who does not know
> That wards the western coast.

St Petroc's Chest, in St Petroc's Church, Bodmin. The Saint's bones were carried off to Brittany by a delinquent monk in 1177, but after a search made in France at the instigation of King Henry II they were found and returned to Bodmin Priory in this ivory casket, thought to have been made by Arab craftsmen in the Norman kingdom of Sicily in the twelfth century.

A window depicting scenes from the life of St Neot in the church at St Neot's, late fifteenth or early sixteenth century. Top row *(left to right): Neot resigns his crown to his younger brother; he takes vows as a monk; he reads the Psalter standing in water, a common penitential practice of Celtic saints; an angel tells him about three fishes in a well: he was to take one only each day, and the supply would never diminish.* Second row: *Neot falls sick and commands his servant to bring him a fish to eat; the servant catches two fishes and cooks them; he brings the meal to Neot; rebuked by his master, the servant throws the fishes into the spring where they are miraculously restored to life.* Third row: *robbers steal Neot's oxen; a man and boy plough his land with stags who offered their services in answer to the Saint's prayers; the oxen are returned to Neot; the Pope blesses St Neot.*

Above: *the 'Mount Cross', of granite, overlooked by the medieval abbey and its nineteenth-century extensions. On the circular head is carved a cross; below that is a figure of Christ with outstretched arms, and another cross which extends down the shaft.*

Opposite: *St Michael's Chair, seen from the roof of the church tower. As an act of faith pilgrims would clamber out over the battlements and sit with their back against the H-like structure of the lantern, their feet on the seaward side – a precipitous seat.*

In the sixth century a Welsh itinerant monk called St Cado is said to have visited the Mount in search of his mother's sister, St Keyne, who had made her pilgrimage thither and become so loved that the inhabitants detained her. Being thirsty he struck the ground with his staff and procured water for himself and those about him; St Keyne gave the new well to the neighbouring people in token of her gratitude for the churches they had dedicated to her. On another occasion she dealt with a plague of adders by turning them into ammonites. The 'Mount Cross', which stands high on the north-east corner of the Mount, is a relic of the later Celtic centuries; and it itself pre-dates by two centuries or more the twelfth-century Benedictine priory which the Abbot of Mont St Michel in France built as a daughter house of his Norman monastery.

From the earliest days, the monastic buildings stood within the walls of the castle which crowns the island. It was besieged in 1193 and again later, during the Wars of the Roses and the English Civil War. The buildings which the visitor sees today date largely from the nineteenth century, but they include the carefully restored church of the monastery. There the pilgrims made their first stop, to pray and make their offerings at three altars. The high altar, which stood between the altars of St Michael and the Crucified Saviour, bore a tabernacle and a box full of relics. The jawbone of St Apollonia could be seen there. This Roman lady had suffered martyrdom in Alexandria for refusing to sacrifice to a pagan idol, her teeth being pulled out one by one as a prelude to her execution. Devout pilgrims suffering from excruciating toothache could touch their own jawbones with this holy relic. Other pilgrims found relief too. On Sunday 14 May 1262, for example, a certain blind woman called Christina, who lived near Glastonbury, came to High Mass and just before the service received back her sight 'by intercession of the Blessed Archangel Michael'. The monks and congregation testified to her cure, which was recorded in an old manuscript found at Avranches. It tells us that many other such miracles occurred in 1262, and doubtless they went on throughout the long history of pilgrimage to the island.

Going out into the daylight, past a celebrated image of St Michael slaying the dragon, the more hardy pilgrims could put their newly fortified faith to the test. In 1602 the poet Richard Carew wrote:

> Who knows not St Michael's Mount and chair
> The Pilgrims' Holy Vaunt
> Both land and island twice a day
> Both fort and port of haunt.

The 'Holy Vaunt' Carew describes elsewhere as 'a bad seat and craggy place called St Michael's chair somewhat dangerous for access and therefore holy for the adventure'. Long before Carew's time, however, the monks had built a stone lantern on the top of the church tower as a lighthouse, which became the second 'St Michael's Chair'. Pilgrims climbed the tower and perched themselves upon the stone 'seat', gazing down a precipitous drop of hundreds of feet. The tradition that the newly-wed husband or wife who sat first in the seat would dominate the partnership links this custom with that of drinking water from St Keyne's Well.

Before crossing to the Mount, possibly while waiting for the tide to ebb and uncover the causeway, the pilgrims may well have visited the chapel of St Catherine. This small medieval building, built on a rocky foundation between the Mount and Marazion, did not survive the Civil War and has left only the name 'Chapel Rock'. Visitors today can see on the left of the causeway a rock pierced by a socket: medieval pilgrims would have knelt briefly at the wooden cross which stood in this hole.

The Celtic saints of Cornwall, such as Petroc of Bodmin, Fimbur of Fowey, Morwenna of Morwenstow and a score of others, have left us little more than their wells, some foundations of their cells, the crosses where the descendants of their converts once gathered, and some colourful legends of their miraculous lives. To us they are almost as insubstantial as the Archangel Michael must have been when those Cornish-speaking fishermen in the fifth century glimpsed him through the spray flaming atop his chosen crag. What speaks to us most in Cornwall are the primitive origins of medieval pilgrimage: sacred springs and wells of fresh water and the holy hill of St Michael's Mount, so mysteriously joined and separated from the mainland, which drew to them religious men and women in joy or need long before the Celtic saints colonized the peninsula with the Christian faith and the memory of their heroic lives.

The East

Ely *St Etheldreda*

According to tradition, St Augustine founded a church among the fens of East Anglia on the Isle of Ely, so called from the great quantities of eels netted in the marshes around it. In 673 Etheldreda, daughter of Anna, King of East Anglia, established a convent on the island and served as its abbess until her death five years later. During her last illness in 679 Queen Etheldreda (or Audrey as she was also known) endured a tumour in her throat, which she interpreted as punishment for her youthful pleasure in wearing splendid necklaces. In the sixteenth and seventeenth centuries ladies often wore in lieu of necklaces cheap silk or lace collars, called 'St Audrey's Lace'. This 'Tawdry Lace', sold at St Audrey's Fair in Ely each year on 17 October, became a byword for cheap finery, and thus the word 'tawdry' eventually entered our language to describe something showy or gaudy but without real value.

About 685 Abbess Sexburga, the Saint's sister, resolved to translate the bones of Etheldreda from their wooden coffin in the common cemetery to a more suitable shrine. She sent some monks by boat to the deserted Roman camp at Grantchester, where they found near the walls a beautifully carved white marble sarcophagus which they took back with much rejoicing. On 17 October 695 the Abbess and nuns saw the miraculously incorrupt body transferred to this new tomb set inside their abbey church.

Later, as the shrine grew in popularity, the community moved the bones again until they finally rested in a tomb surrounded by those of St Sexburga to the east, St Ermenilda, her niece, to the south, and St Werburga (the latter's sister) to the north – a veritable family of shrines. The fine six-bay presbytery built by Bishop Northwold in the thirteenth century to house the shrines and provide more room for pilgrims can still be seen. Here Henry III, his son Edward and a noble concourse witnessed the last translation of the relics in 1252.

The fame of Etheldreda and Werburga as saints depended in part upon the discovery of the incorruption of their bodies. A chronicler writing about the translation of the latter to Ely noted that 'indeed her body appeared as fair as though she had just been dead'. To the medieval mind it seemed that their condition typified the state of final incorruption, conclusive evidence of their sanctity. 'Nowhere could be found so many saints entire after death', wrote William of Malmesbury proudly about his native land.

Nothing now remains of the white marble tomb, the silver reliquary or the treasure house of jewels and coins given by grateful pilgrims who knelt at the shrine of St Etheldreda, but a few fragments of the shrine survive. And some reputed relics of the Saint are beneath the altar of the Roman Catholic church of St Etheldreda in Ely Place, London – formerly the chapel of the London palace of the bishops of Ely – and in the Roman Catholic church at Ely.

In Ely Cathedral itself a series of medieval sculptures depicting the life of St Etheldreda escaped the zeal of both Thomas Cromwell and his namesake Oliver in the following century. It forms a fitting memorial to one of the most popular saints of East Anglia. Also a pair of mid-fifteenth-century panels

Opposite: *a scene from the life of St Etheldreda, carved on a capital in the Octagon of Ely Cathedral (c. 1325): the miracle at St Abb's Head. Pursued by her second husband, King Egfrid of Northumbria, she had fled from her convent at Coldingham towards her lands at Ely. She took refuge from his men on the headland, which was promptly cut off from the mainland for a week by miraculous high seas. Before they had subsided Egfrid wearied of the siege and left her in peace.*

The reputed hand of St Etheldreda, found on the Duke of Norfolk's estate at Arundel in Sussex, can be seen in the Roman Catholic church of St Etheldreda at Ely.

The life of St Etheldreda, from an altarpiece. The scenes depicted are: The marriage of Etheldreda to King Egfrid in 660; Etheldreda taking leave of him to retire to a convent; the Saint building her first church at Ely; and the removal of her body to a stone coffin in 695. (Society of Antiquaries, London).

Opposite: *the retrochoir of Ely Cathedral, where the shrine of St Etheldreda once stood. The tomb-like structure on the left contains fragments of the shrine.*

showing four scenes from Etheldreda's life survive, having been discovered in the late eighteenth century doing service as a cupboard door in a cottage at Ely. They probably formed part of an altarpiece in the abbey church, and may even have been the wings of the golden and jewelled retable before the shrine itself. In the last picture the Saint's incorrupt body is being lowered into a marble coffin, which may well be a representation of that early Roman sarcophagus found at Grantchester.

SAINT AND
WHO FOUNDED
A.D
673

Bury St Edmunds *St Edmund*

The Scandinavian freebooters who from the eighth century onwards harried the east coast, sailing up the river estuaries in their long ships, fought many battles against the Saxon defenders. In 869 they captured King Edmund of East Anglia. Rather than accept freedom in exchange for denying Christ, the young Saxon chose a martyr's death. On 20 November in that doleful year the Danes tied him to a tree and threw their spears at him (later stories say arrows), 'as if in sport'. When he still remained faithful they cut off his head and, as a final humiliation, hid it in a thicket in the dense wood at Eglesdene, so that it might not be buried.

After the Danes had broken camp the local Saxons searched for the head of their slain master. Edmund's early biographer says that a voice calling 'Here! Here! Here!' led them to the thicket, where they found a wolf guarding the head against other wild animals. This beast allowed them to carry away the head to Hoxne (or possibly Sutton, near Woodbridge) for burial, following meekly in their steps. Thus a wolf became one of the badges or emblems of St Edmund.

In 903 monks removed the body, now miraculously one again, to a wooden church at Beodricsworth, later Bury St Edmunds. After fleeing to London for safety when a fresh wave of Danish invaders menaced the township, they returned the relics and installed them in their unfinished stone church. On their way home they rested the bier in the little wooden Saxon church at Greensted-juxta-Ongar in Essex, whose thick vertically-set timbers stand to this day. On St Luke's Day 1032 the shrine was consecrated in the presence of King Canute, who offered the Saint a votive gold crown from his own brow. After the Conquest, the Normans rebuilt the abbey church, and in 1095 St Edmund's relics were installed in the presbytery behind the high altar.

Throughout East Anglia and wider afield the fame of St Edmund, King and Martyr, spread as the Middle Ages unfolded. More than fifty churches, such as Southwold Church in Suffolk, are dedicated to him; his statue or painted image on wall or screen adorns many others. Kings, nobles and commoners flocked to his shrine at Bury and drank the healing Water of St Edmund. From Canute onwards monarchs worshipped at the tomb of the young King who had lost his life in defence of England and the Christian faith. Edward the Confessor came here often, usually walking the last mile on foot. When Henry VI made his pilgrimage to Bury in 1433 the monks presented him with a beautifully illustrated *Life* of St Edmund by one of their number, John Lydgate.

St Edmund's relics still fought the wars of their erstwhile owner. According to Roger de Horeden, King Sweyn met an untimely end in 1014 because he doubted Edmund's sanctity and threatened the town. While ensconced on his throne mouthing his

Below: *the wolf guarding St Edmund's head: an illustration from the manuscript of Lydgate's* Lives of Saints Edmund and Fremund *presented to King Henry VI in 1433. (British Library, London, Harley MS 2278)*

Opposite: *The church at Greensted-juxta-Ongar. The timber nave is Anglo-Saxon in date, probably late tenth-century: its walls consist of massive tree-trunks, split in two and set vertically.*

intentions he saw the warrior Saint advancing upon him brandishing a spear. Shouting out that Edmund had come to slay him he toppled off his seat and lay in a coma for three days until death released him. For speaking disparagingly of Edmund's memory and sauntering around the shrine a Danish nobleman called Osgoth received the affliction of madness. Thus medieval people were taught to respect and even fear the power of a saint's relics. Plenty of stories vividly described the consequences of not doing so.

Most shrines kept a book recording miracles, and many people could testify to the miraculous favours of St Edmund. When Samson, Abbot from 1182 to 1212, compiled the Bury book three Londoners came to him and insisted upon appearing in it as St Edmund had once sent them a favourable wind on a voyage to St Gilles. Clearly the awareness of having been involved in a miracle enhanced their sense of personal worth, and they were determined to enter the fact into the history books. An old blind man from Northumber-

land recovered his sight when the party of pilgrims he accompanied had come within sight of the high bell-tower of the abbey church and knelt in prayer. Dunwich fishermen caught in a storm hung up an anchor of wax at the shrine as token of their safe delivery. But a Fleming who pretended to kiss the feretory while trying to lick up a gold piece left on it found his lips glued there all day until he confessed and was set free by the Saint.

Rather strangely, people believed that Edmund's relics could induce fertility. Even in Tudor times married women in Bury who wanted to bear a child enacted a curious rite on 20 November, the day of St Edmund's chief festival. Accompanied by a column of monks they processed as far as the monastery gate walking beside a white bull and stroking its flanks. The Oblation of the White Bull continued as the women left the beast behind and went to the Saint's shrine where they made their offerings, uttered their vows and asked for the grace of St Edmund in their need.

The climax of any medieval pilgrimage often came during the Saint's festival, when the streets of the town would be decked out for a fair. Both inside churches and on the streets, actors drawn from the townsfolk performed miracle plays. At Chester, for example, Adam and Eve appeared naked on the stage, while Noah told his spouse that he was 'off to fetch a new wife'. But these festivities could cause trouble. In 1197 the servants of the abbey at Bury quarrelled with the burgesses over certain plays and a riot ensued. As a result a hundred townsmen had to make amends by submitting their naked backs to penitential rods wielded by the monks at the abbey door. The crowds who thronged to the Bury Fair also attracted pickpockets and cutpurses. One year Deorman, a rich merchant of London, brought his silks and spices for sale at Bury. As he prayed at the tomb a woman cut away his bulky purse and made her escape. Deorman protested to St Edmund. Going out of the church door he unknowingly set his hand on the thief: she confessed and restored all, so Deorman let her go free. Some time later he became a monk at Bury, spending the rest of his days near the relics which had once safeguarded his earthly treasures.

The most striking remains of the great abbey today are two entrances into its precincts – the tall, severe Norman Gate, finished about 1150, and the exquisitely decorated Gothic Great Gate, added some two hundred years later, after the abbey had been invaded and damaged by rioters during the troubles that preceded the deposition of Edward II in 1327.

Opposite: *the Great Gate of St Edmund's Abbey.* Below: *The entombment of St Edmund at Bury. The lid of the tomb is raised, suggesting how the canopies of shrines could be lifted by systems of wires and pulleys. (From Lydgate's* Lives of Saints Edmund and Fremund. *British Library, London, Harley MS 2278)*

Norfolk *St William of Norwich and St Walstan of Bawburgh*

Bishop Herbert de Losinga saw the foundation stone of Norwich Cathedral laid in 1096, and before his death in 1119 the eastern parts of the great building had taken the shape we see today. They included a chapel dedicated to the Holy Martyrs (now the Jesus Chapel), where the bones of St William of Norwich once rested. Near the chapel there is a low arch built across the aisle like a bridge, reached by a spiral staircase, from where relics could be viewed. In the painted vault above the bridge are pictures of twelve saints around Christ in Majesty; the Disciples are also shown in a faded mural on the arch west of the bridge. (This bridge now houses a display of the cathedral's treasures.)

St William was a boy of twelve, apprenticed to a skinner in Norwich since the age of eight, when he met a violent death in 1140. According to a most unreliable legend, the local Jews tortured and crucified him in a ritual murder and hid the body in Thorpe Wood. (The same anti-semitic legend is the basis of the story of Little St Hugh of Lincoln: see p. 136.) The deed discovered, the Bishop ordered the boy's body to be reinterred, first in the monks' cemetery, then in the chapter-house. Subsequently it was moved into the cathedral.

Thomas of Monmouth, a monk of the priory, mentions large numbers of pilgrims who came thither for healing. A dumb seven-year-old brought by his parents kissed the stone sepulchre holding a lighted candle and uttered his first words, 'asking that he might go back home'.

Clearly the growing numbers of common pilgrims treated the shrine with familiarity, for Thomas records a convenient appearance by the Saint in a vision to an unnamed man. 'Be thou my messenger,' the boy martyr told him, 'and on next Sunday go to my sepulchre, and there proclaim to those present that more reverence must be shown to me than heretofore. For some presume to touch the stone of my sepulchre, or the cloth, with muddy feet, nay, even to soil it; and the pavement around me is defiled with the foul spittle of many. Be careful, then, to warn my Thomas that he take greater care of my tomb.' Yet Thomas on a later occasion could not stop a woman called Wimar of Bardney from vomiting violently on the pavement: the bystanders rushed out, leaving the sacrists to cleanse the spot and strew it with fragrant herbs. Being cured, she journeyed to Rome to tell her story to the Pope.

The catalogue of miracles includes the usual deliverances from storms at sea, recovery of livestock, and restoration of sight to the blind, power of walking to the lame and sense to the insane. Thomas of York, who hobbled for many days all the way from that city to Norwich on a pair of crutches, left them at St William's shrine as a votive offering. Yet there are stories which stretch our credulity. For example, there is the tale of a youth of Hellington, a village about seven miles from Norwich, who fell asleep while minding his father's herd and swallowed an adder which had crept into his gaping mouth. After days of torment he drank water made holy by scrapings from the sepulchre; then he rushed out of the church and vomited up the serpent with its two young ones on the grass before the doors.

Philip de Bella Arbore, a native of Lorraine, noble by birth and a soldier by profession, made an unusual spectacle in the cathedral even in those days. For a fratricide which included burning a church and its inmates he was sentenced by the Pope to a penance of ten years of wandering pilgrimage clothed in a shirt of mail on his bare flesh, girt with his sword, and his arms ringed with iron bands. After seven years of such exile Philip found his first mercy at Jerusalem where in the church of the Holy Sepulchre his mail shirt burst asunder. In like manner in Ireland at St Brendan's shrine (at Clonfert, though no trace of it now remains) the sword broke in pieces. When after long wanderings he had traversed most parts of England seeking the prayers of the saints at their shrines, he came to Norwich where before the sepulchre of St William the iron on his right arm suddenly snapped, startling the bystanders with its sound.

Another wandering penitent found a similar relief at Norwich. Glewus, a Lincolnshire man, killed his brother with an iron pitchfork. Condemned to banishment, he donned a hair shirt and made a ring of the murderous iron pitchfork and put it round the right arm with which he had slain his brother. For three years he visited shrines throughout England to obtain mercy until at Bury St Edmunds the iron ring cracked but still remained in place, one end biting into his arm. At Norwich, however, the ring broke on the other side and fell away. The Bishop himself came to the spot and led a hymn of praise.

Yet Thomas of Monmouth saved his best story until last. In 1172 Gaufrid of Canterbury was afflicted with a severe toothache and had three teeth out. Foolishly he then sat down to a supper of white peas and a fat goose with garlic, washed down by new ale. His head swelled up hideously, and his friends had to insert a reed into his mouth to enable him to breathe. They took him to Becket's tomb to spend the night there, and he saw the Saint in a dream. St Thomas asked him

The Jesus Chapel in Norwich Cathedral, an early site of St William's shrine, north of the apse. The windows are later insertions or enlargements in Norman walls.

what he sought: Gaufrid replied that he wanted to recover. 'Thy healing is not here,' said St Thomas, 'but, lest thou be deprived of all profit from coming to me, I will give thee counsel. Rise, then, and return home: make a candle in the name of St William the martyr of Norwich; put it all about thy head and thou shalt receive speedy relief: when thou art healed, hasten to Norwich and offer that candle to thy liberator.' Gaufrid carried out the instructions and was cured. At Ospringe on his way to Norwich he prayed for good companions on his pilgrimage and was miraculously joined by St Thomas Becket and St Edmund, who left him three miles short of Bury after revealing their identity. At Norwich he offered the candle and threepence, and also told Thomas of Monmouth his tale. Thomas went to Canterbury to verify the story, and found confirmation of the wonderful speed of his journey, namely that 'he started from Canterbury on one day and arrived at Norwich on the next'.

Norfolk possessed many other shrines to local saints in the Middle Ages. Some of them seem to have provided cover for a continuation of the old pagan religion. St Walstan of Bawburgh, five miles west of Norwich, may have replaced some ancient cattle-god in the popular religion, for he became the patron saint of husbandmen and beasts, and is usually depicted holding a scythe. Born at Bawburgh, Walstan worked on a farm at Taverham a few miles away. The farmer offered to make the pious plough lad his heir, but Walstan would accept only two ox-calves. Warned by an angel of his impending death in 1016 Walstan prayed for all sick creatures, both man and beast. He died in the fields, and his body was drawn to Bawburgh Church by his two oxen, who reputedly passed over the River Wensum without wetting their hooves and entered the church through a wall which opened miraculously for them.

Where they paused on their way three holy wells appeared. One of them still exists as a healing spring and attracts pilgrims annually to it. It can be seen today in an orchard near the church, not far from a Slipper House where the Norfolk farmers and herdsmen left their shoes before completing their pilgrimage on behalf of themselves and their animals at the shrine itself.

The Reliquary Arch in Norwich Cathedral, built about 1424 as an ante-chapel to the Reliquary Chapel which once stood nearby, outside the now-blocked pointed arch on the left.

Crowland *St Guthlac*

Crowland is a market town in Lincolnshire, about eight miles north-east of Peterborough. Thanks to centuries of draining the town now stands on dry agricultural land; but in the Middle Ages the fens stretched for mile after mile under a great East Anglian sky, meres of water interspersed with thick beds of reeds. In the eighth century this forbidding swamp formed the backcloth of the life of St Guthlac the Hermit.

Born into the Mercian royal family, Guthlac at first followed a soldier's course until, like Saul of Tarsus, he experienced a sudden conversion and returned to become a monk at Repton. Then he resolved to live as a hermit and made his way eastwards to the wild wasteland of the fens. He paddled and poled himself along in a punt until he found a small island called Crowland, or Croyland as it appears in early writings. There, on a tumulus where a hole had been scooped out by treasure-seekers, he built his hut. The rough stone foundations of walls and piers suggest that it became a spacious cell. Indeed there is mention of a church and servants during his lifetime, and so he must have attracted a small community of fellow hermits who possibly lived on the high ground to the south-east, joined by a causeway, where the later abbey of Croyland was built.

Guthlac wore animal skins and fasted severely, taking only a morsel of barley bread and some cups of muddy water after sunset. There is a remarkable medieval roll of pictures of his life (now in the British Library); it shows him, for instance, being rescued from three days of despair by a miraculous visit from St Bartholomew. The devils who inhabited the stinking bogs and green-mantled pools around Crowland gave him no respite until his death in 714, and Guthlac's fame rested upon his vigorous resistance to their temptations. Another scene depicts the visit of Ethelbald, later King of Mercia, who came during his exile to seek the Saint's intercession.

Two years after Guthlac's death an abbey was founded on the site of his hermitage and grave. The church, which rose on piles driven into the fens, was several times rebuilt and remodelled over the centuries. There pilgrims continued to pray for the healing powers of St Guthlac, whose fame as a physician spread beyond the borders of Lincolnshire throughout East Anglia and the Midlands. The striking west front which greeted them, with its mid-thirteenth-century carved roundels of the life of the Saint, its vast window and its massive late Gothic tower, stands in skeletal form for the visitor today.

The west front of Crowland Abbey.

Scenes from the life of St Guthlac, from the Guthlac Roll, *possibly painted at Crowland Abbey* c. *1200. (1) The Saint being ferried to Crowland; (2) he builds a church there; (3) assailed by demons, he is rescued from the jaws of hell by St Bartholomew. (British Library, London, Harley MS Y.6)*

Walsingham *England's Nazareth*

As ye came from the holy land
of Walsinghame,
Met you not with my true love
By the way as you came

How should I know your true love,
That have met many a one
As I came from the holy land
That have come, that have gone?

Anon., *c.* 1510

In the early twelfth century a widow of good family and some wealth named Richelde de Faverches lived in the village of Little Walsingham near the north coast of Norfolk. She venerated Our Lady, and one day saw her in a vision. The Virgin Mary showed her the little house in Nazareth where the Archangel Gabriel had announced his joyful news and where she had lived while bringing up the boy Jesus. In the vision, repeated on two other occasions, the mother of the Saviour directed Richelde to note the dimensions of it so that she could build a replica in Norfolk.

With the help of the village craftsmen Richelde obeyed these instructions, but then hesitated about where to site the wooden structure. That morning the sparkling dew covered an adjoining meadow but left two dry patches some seventy paces apart. Interpreting this phenomenon as a divine sign, Richelde ordered the workmen to erect the House on the patch nearest to two holy wells. They could not fasten it properly upon its foundations, for it seemed that the House did not want to be built there. That night, while the dispirited workmen slept and Richelde prayed, angels removed it to the second patch 'two hundred fote and more in dystaunce'.

Richelde built a stone church some twenty-three by thirteen feet in size around the wooden House, and her son Geoffrey eventually endowed it with land. His chaplain Edwy founded the first religious house there. Later, returning crusaders brought a phial containing reputed milk from the breast of the Virgin Mary. In all probability it held white dust picked up from the floor of the cave of Our Lady's Milk in Bethlehem. In time the more credulous people even came to believe that the spirit of the Mother of Jesus had abandoned her haunts in the Holy Land when the infidels conquered it, and had settled down in Norfolk. In the reign of Edward III the Augustinians or Black Canons acquired custody of the shrine and built a splendid priory around it.

Like the shrine of Becket, the House of Mary at Walsingham attracted pilgrims from all over England and Europe. Pilgrims from the North would pass through King's Lynn, which was also one of the principal ports where foreign pilgrims landed, and possibly rest at the priories of Flitcham and Rudham beyond the town. Of the many inns and chapels which once stood beside this particular pilgrim road there are but few remains today. Yet the Chapel of the Red Mount, halfway between the south and east gates of King's Lynn, is by far the most complete and impressive example of a pilgrim wayside chapel in this country. Built by Robert Corraunce in 1485, the red-brick octagonal tower contains a little cruciform chapel with a fan-vaulted roof, lit by four quatrefoil windows. Beneath it there is a vestry or priest's living room with another small chapel, and below yet a third chapel, all for the use of pilgrims bound for Walsingham. The building was dedicated to St Mary, and pilgrims commonly called it Our Lady's Mount or St Mary-on-the Hill. Probably they resorted there to give thanks for a safe voyage and to make their confession, a desirable preliminary before a pilgrimage.

The four religious houses in King's Lynn would have provided hospitality for the pilgrims. The lantern tower of the Greyfriars' church still stands in the town, as do gateways of the Austin (Augustinian) Friars and Whitefriars, but only a street name indicates the site of the house of the Blackfriars. St Margaret's Church, founded in about 1140 by the first Bishop of Norwich, once formed part of a priory. It contains two great brasses of former mayors, both of whom must have made their pilgrimage to Walsingham: Adam de Walsoken (died 1349), in plain loose coat with sleeves and hood, and Robert Braunche (died 1364). Adam and his wife Margaret kneel in prayer under richly ornamented arches, with angels at their shoulders. Angels with musical instruments occupy niches in the sides of the canopy, and two panels below depict scenes of everyday country life: men gathering apples, a farmer with a sack of corn on his back riding towards a windmill. The panel beneath Robert Braunche and his two wives shows a fourteenth-century feast in full swing, the guests seated at a table full of dishes and attended by serving ladies and musicians.

King's Lynn also saw the birth of a remarkable pilgrim, one of the few known to us as an individual: Margery Kempe, daughter of John of Brunham, five times Mayor of Lynn. She wrote the first known autobiography in the English language, and so we can trace her steps through life with some confidence. At the age of twenty she married John Kempe of Lynn, to whom she bore fourteen children. She then saw visions, and agreed with her husband that she should go on a pilgrimage. After visiting the shrines of England she journeyed to the Holy Land. Her loud penitential weeping and continuous religious devotions usually proved too much for the companies of pilgrims she joined on her travels. In 1414, when she

The Red Mount Chapel, King's Lynn.

reached Jerusalem, Margery wrote that she 'could not keep herself from crying and roaring though she should have died of it'. Two years later she went to Compostela, and after returning to England she sailed again for Danzig. By now she travelled alone. After landing at Dover on her return she walked to London in sackcloth. In her story, Margery described how 'this creature' (as she called herself) spoke out like a true prophet against the vice she saw in the London streets, adding with some satisfaction that 'her speaking profited right much in many persons'.

Not all Londoners, however, lived such worldly lives that they never made the pilgrimage to Walsingham. Their most direct route would take them along the Icknield Way through Royston, Newmarket, Brandon, Swaffham and Fakenham. At the hamlet of Hilborough, between Brandon and Swaffham, an ivy-covered ruined wall of a pilgrim chapel stands in a field not far from this road. Pilgrims from the south crossed the River Nar at Newton, close to Castle Acre where the Peddar's Way branched towards Hunstanton. William de Warenne, who married Gundrada the Conqueror's daughter, built the castle and added a priory after returning from a pilgrimage to Rome. Today the Tudor gatehouse of the priory leads into a site covering no less than thirty-six acres. Here the pilgrims once inspected the priory's chief relic, an arm of St Philip. The little altar in the small infirmary

Castle Acre: from left to right, the west front of the church, the prior's house and the inner gatehouse.

chapel, where poor pilgrims too old and weak to reach Walsingham would have received the Last Sacrament before dying, still stands among the ruins. Pilgrims of higher social status may well have stayed in the prior's house, which survives complete with gabled roof, oriel windows, and a chapel in the upper storey beneath heavy oak beams.

Having crossed the River Wensum at Fakenham and breasted a hill the pilgrims dipped down to East Barsham where a bridge took them over the River Stiffkey. Here King Henry VIII dismounted before continuing on foot to Little Walsingham, over two miles away, to pray for the life of his and Catherine of Aragon's infant son. Like most pilgrims, when he reached Houghton St Giles, on a low hill a mile further on, the King took off his shoes and walked barefoot the rest of the way. The fine fourteenth-century pilgrim chapel, once converted into a cottage but now restored and rededicated, is still known as the 'Shoe House' or 'Slipper Chapel', for there the pilgrims removed their shoes. In the parish church nearby, also built of Norfolk flint, there is an old screen painted with pictures of women saints, the Virgin Mary – the goal of the pilgrims to Walsingham – and the four Latin doctors, but the sword points of Cromwellian troopers have scratched out the faces. By now the pilgrims on the long almost straight road from the south, weary of the endless sandy heaths and dark woods of Norfolk, would feel a growing excitement. Like the Magi of old, the first pilgrims, they were drawing near to the Mother and Child. Just as the Wise Men had followed a star, so these pilgrims called the galaxy of stars we call the Milky Way by a new name, the 'Walsingham Way', because it seemed to their eyes to hover over the sacred House and to guide their footsteps on their journey.

Some pilgrims, however, would approach Walsingham from the east, having been to see the Holy Rood in Bromholm Priory, whose ruins lie near the village of Bacton on the coast about twenty-six miles away. Until the early thirteenth century Bromholm, a daughter house of the great Norman abbey at Castle Acre, enjoyed a decent obscurity. But then it acquired a famous relic, a piece of the True Cross. Matthew Paris, the thirteenth-century historian and monk of St Alban's, narrated its supposed history. It had belonged to the crusaders; after the sack of Constantinople in 1204 an English chaplain brought it to England. He offered his collection of looted relics to several monasteries, disposing of some jewelled crosses and two fingers of St Margaret to St Alban's Abbey, but the great religious houses turned down his cross 'made from two transverse pieces of wood of about the length of a man's hand'. But Bromholm Priory then accepted him as a member – 'as well as his two children' – and at once the relic began to work such miracles as raising the dead to life, cleansing lepers, restoring sight and exorcising those possessed by demons.

When news spread of the miracles wrought in this remote corner of Norfolk for a short time Bromholm rivalled Canterbury in popularity. In 1466 the corpse of John Paston lay there, and 'the reek of the torches of the dirge was so overpowering that the priory glazier had to remove two panes of glass so that the mourners should not be suffocated.' The miller's wife in Chaucer's 'Reeve's Tale' speaks for the nameless multitude of pilgrims when out of her sleep she exclaims 'Help, Holy Cross of Bromeholm!' Besides badges or tokens, pilgrims could buy devotional cards at many medieval shrines, and by chance one of those sold at Bromholm has survived, stuck to a page in a fourteenth-century *Hours of the Virgin* in Lambeth Palace Library. On the sides are the words:

> This cross yat here peynted is
> Signe of ye cros of bromholm is

Illuminated devotional card of the Holy Rood at Bromholm. (Lambeth Palace Library, London, MS 545)

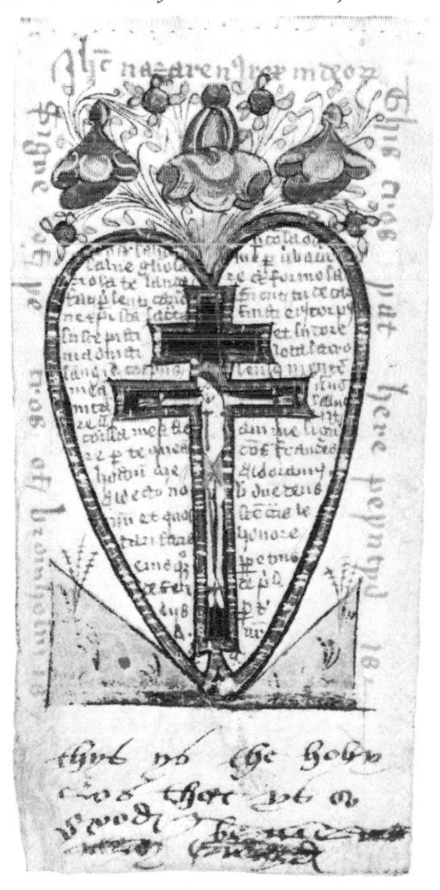

The 'Slipper Chapel' at Houghton St Giles, c.1350.

Beneath the patriarchal cross superimposed on a heart and filled with the words of a Latin hymn written in minute letters and entitled *Jhesus Nazarenus Rex Judeorum*, someone has added in another hand:

> This is the holy cros that ys so spede
> He[ar] me in my need

Pilgrims who could afford a sea passage to Walsingham might have disembarked seven miles to the north of it at Wells-next-the-Sea, then a small fishing harbour at the mouth of a river estuary. They may have stayed the night four miles away at Binham Priory, the nave of which still does service as the parish church. Prior Richard de Parco's richly arcaded west front, built about the year 1240, survives complete with bellcote beyond the ruined gatehouse. Inside the Norman nave the medieval screen shows some traces of its gallery of saints. Founded by a nephew of the Conqueror as an outlying house of St Alban's Abbey, Binham must have gained both wealth and reflected glory from its proximity to Walsingham.

Besides kings, nobles and the Norfolk gentry, many thousands of common pilgrims made their way to Walsingham. The late fourteenth-century writer Langland mentions them in his *Vision of Piers Plowman*. Between the hill-top of Truth and the deep valley of Falsehood the poet saw the world as being like a great plain, with men and women living their worldly lives:

Pilgrims and palmers plighted them together
To see St James, and saints in Rome.
They went forth in their way with many wise tales.
And had leave to lie all their life after . . .
Hermits on an heap, with hooked staves,
Went to Walsingham, and their wenches after;
Great lubbers and long, that loth were to labour,
Clothed them in capes to be known from other,
And shaped themselves as hermits, their ease to have.

Piers Plowman, both the dreamer and the hero of the poem, paints a picture of the Seven Deadly Sins confessing themselves to Repentance under the promptings of Reason. Avarice, for example, admits to giving short weights, watered beer and false measure, but swears that he will purge himself of sin's consequences by a pilgrimage to Walsingham with his wife Alise and that he will also 'byd the roode of Broomholme bring me out of dette'.

From north, south, east and west the barefooted pilgrims finally converged on Walsingham and made their way through the main street lined with inns. Here they caught sight of the priory gatehouse, through which they passed under the watchful gaze of monks alert for potential relic-snatchers. Inside the precincts the pilgrim entered the small chapel of St Lawrence where a monk offered him a bone, said to be the finger-bone of St Peter, for him to kiss. A guide then led him to a thatched building over the two holy wells containing 'wonderfully cold' water which not only healed headache and stomach pains but also could grant the pilgrim's wishes. A book of instructions to the guardians of the wells, which belonged to Prior Richard Vowell in the fifteenth century, enjoined them to see that no one bathed alone, and that no sick pilgrim immersed himself without permission from a physician. The tank used for bathing, which can still be seen, was obviously too deep for safety. After the Reformation the springs that fed the bath survived as wishing wells. The aspirant for a boon knelt with right knee bared on a stone between them and plunged a hand into each while making his wish, which he then washed down with as much water from both springs as he could hold in the hollow of his hands. His wish would be granted within a year if in the meantime he refrained from uttering it aloud to others or even himself. Pilgrims might carry away this wonder-working water for their friends and relatives in lead *ampullae*; and small hollow flasks, often bearing the stamp of a letter W with a crown over it, would be sewn through two perforated lugs to a hat or garment, as a sign of the pilgrimage. At Walsingham pilgrims could also buy brooches (secured by pin and clasp) showing the Virgin Mary.

Walsingham pilgrim badge showing the Annunciation, fourteenth century. (Museum of London)

Next the pilgrim made his way through a narrow wicket-gate called the Knight's Gate. According to tradition, in 1314 Sir Ralph de Boutetort rode hard for sanctuary at Walsingham hotly pursued by his enemies. Mounted and in full armour he could not get through the wicket-gate, nor did he have time to dismount. He breathed a prayer to Our Lady of Walsingham who obligingly let him through. A copper plaque of a knight on horseback over the gate commemorated the miracle for the benefit of pilgrims. The gateway, less the plaque, still exists, although it has been moved a small distance to the south of its original position. Once through the Knight's Gate the pilgrim at last found himself in a courtyard in front of the Lady Chapel, the stone building containing the House of Nazareth.

'The church is neat and elegant', wrote Erasmus, who visited the shrine in 1512, 'but the Virgin dwells not in it . . . The building is not finished, and the breeze comes in at the doors and windows, for the ocean, father of winds, is nearby.' Once inside the chapel, a door let into each side of the small, narrow wooden House allowed a constant one-way procession of pilgrims to pass through it. On the right of the altar, shrouded in a perpetual haze of incense, stood the ancient and renowned statue of the Virgin. If the priory seal depicts it accurately, Mary sat crowned upon a throne with the Holy Child upon her knee. She held a lily-sceptre in her hand, while a toadstone, a symbol of evil, lay vanquished under her feet. By the light of sweet-smelling tapers Erasmus saw that the place was

The modern Anglican shrine of Our Lady, in a re-creation of the Holy House.

Our Lady of Walsingham, depicted on the thirteenth-century seal of the priory. (British Library, London)

'meet for saints, all things be so bright with gold, silver and precious stones'. He thought the statue 'of no extraordinary size, material or workmanship, but in virtue most efficacious'. After kneeling in prayer each pilgrim made his offering, and a priest immediately scooped it up to prevent any theft. Next the pilgrim entered the priory church to see the crystal phial of Mary's milk, in a reliquary on the high altar. Erasmus describes the 'milk' as moist but congealed, like chalk mixed with white of egg. After praying to share the 'happy childhood' of Jesus and to grow in Christ fed on 'the true milk of the Gospel' Erasmus noted that 'the holy Milk seemed to leap a little, and the Eucharist shone somewhat brighter.' The attendant thrust forward a small hollowed slab of wood, 'such as those used by toll-collectors on bridges in Germany'. The scholar paid his due. Then, after seeing the indulgence of forty days, he was shown 'the Virgin's most secret treasures' by the Sub-Prior.

Yet the 'Blessed Mary' at Walsingham had her rivals. Erasmus's friend Sir Thomas More overheard this snatch of conversation: ' "of all Our Ladies, I love best Our Lady of Walsingham", "and I," saith the other, "Our Lady of Ipswich" '.

At the Dissolution the King's men burnt the statue of Our Lady of Walsingham at Smithfield in London, in company with other images of the Virgin Mary from Islington, Ipswich and Doncaster. Gradually Walsingham lapsed back into obscurity as a remote Norfolk village, but the memory of great days lingered on. An anonymous lament found among the papers of Philip, Earl of Arundel, who died in the Tower in 1595, included these lines:

> Bitter, bitter, oh to behold the grass to grow,
> Where the walls of Walsingham so stately did show
> Level, level with the ground the towers do lie
> Which with their golden glittering tops pierced once
> to the sky
> Where were gates, no gates are now; the ways unknown,
> Where the press of peers did pass while her fame far
> was blown.
> Owls do shriek where the sweetest hymns lately
> were sung,
> Toads and serpents hold their dens where the palmers
> did throng.
> Weep, weep O Walsingham, whose days are nights,
> Blessing turned to blasphemies, holy deeds to despites.
> Sin is where our Lady sat, heaven turned is to hell,
> Satan sits where our Lord did sway, Walsingham oh
> farewell.

Yet the story of Walsingham as a place of pilgrimage does not end upon this sad note. In the nineteenth century the Tractarian movement in the Church of England and the restoration of the Roman Catholic hierarchy paved the way for two renewals of the historic pilgrimage. In 1931 some Anglo-Catholics began to build a replica of the medieval Holy House just beyond the ruined priory walls, on the north side, where the presence of medieval stonework and a well – possibly the 'Cabbokeswell' mentioned in a deed of 1380 – suggested the possible site of the old almonry. Three years later the Roman Catholics opened the Slipper Chapel at Houghton St Giles as a shrine to Our Lady of Walsingham. Thus every year thousands of pilgrims still crowd the streets of Walsingham. The Anglicans visit a replica of the statue of Mary and the Holy House encased in an ornate baroque red-brick church facing the Knight's Gate in the old walls. Before leaving, pilgrims are offered a drink from the well, which is clearly regarded as a holy well. For their part, the Roman Catholics worship in the Slipper Chapel and then process to the supposed site of the original Holy House in the precincts of the priory. Near the walled garden of the Anglican church live two anchorites, both nuns, as recluses – solitary survivors of a medieval vocation, their lives dedicated to prayer, in their rooms behind high hedges.

In 1961 Pope John XXIII promised the guardian of the Anglican shrine in an audience that he would say Mass for Walsingham and give his blessing to all who visited it. He might have chosen his prayer from a verse history of Walsingham published in 1496 by Richard Pynson (one of the earliest works of printing in England):

> Therefore blessed Lady, grant thou thy great grace
> To all that thee devoutedly visit in this place.

The Midlands

The Saxon crypt of St Wystan's Church, at Repton, Derbyshire. Originally a royal mausoleum, it became the centre of the cult of St Wystan, grandson of the King of Mercia, when miracles followed his murder in 850. In the end his relics were divided between Evesham Abbey and a shrine here, between four monolithic spiral-carved columns.

Oxford *St Frideswide and others*

In the eighth century Didanus, a Mercian ruler of Oxford, allowed his daughter Frideswide to become a nun, and built for her and twelve other young virgin novices a religious house on the southern edge of the city. After his death Algar, a prince of Leicester, sought to abduct her for his matrimonial bed. Warned of this impending fate in a dream Frideswide fled to a riverside retreat called Bentona. Blindness afflicted both his envoys and Algar himself when he came to Oxford to remove his unwilling victim, although the prayers of the compassionate Frideswide later healed them.

Scholars have argued over the location of Bentona, but one tradition identifies Binsey as the place where Frideswide rested with her companions during their exile from Oxford. In this wild tangle of forest the Saint prayed to God for water, and a pure spring welled up at her feet. Here she made an oratory, and worked miracles of healing. Subsequently, covered by a small stone house, it became one of the most celebrated holy wells in the land. It is said that the village of Seacourt on the other bank of the river once contained no less than twenty-two inns built to accommodate the pilgrims who flocked to St Frideswide's Well.

When she died the nuns buried her body in the church of her Oxford priory. Fire destroyed the church while it sheltered some marauding Danes in 1002, but Ethelbert rebuilt it two years later and placed the Saint's shrine in the centre. By 1122 the Augustinian Canons had acquired the priory and after years of reconstructing the church, in 1180, they translated the relics again with great ceremony. Henry III, Edward I and Catherine of Aragon all made their pilgrimages to the shrine. After the Reformation, however, the Saint's bones were removed from Christ Church Cathedral, as the priory church of St Frideswide had become, in Christ Church College. Under Edward VI the remains of a former nun who married Peter Martyr, Regius Professor of Divinity, lay in or beside the shrine, but in Queen Mary's reign they were relegated to a grave near the Dean's stables and those of Frideswide restored to their rightful place. Queen Elizabeth's episcopal commission of inquiry produced a characteristic compromise: the bones of St Frideswide and Catherine were mixed up and buried in one grave beneath the Lady Chapel. The marble shrine in which her relics were installed in 1289 has been partly reconstructed from fragments and now commemorates the Saxon Saint; she is still honoured on 19 October by special services and a procession to the stone slab west of the shrine which covers her reputed bones.

Below and opposite: *the shrine of St Frideswide in Oxford Cathedral.*

A mutilated face in a nun's wimple in the centre of the north side of the shrine may represent St Frideswide, while those on the south side may be intended for Katherine and Cicely, two nuns who fled with her to Binsey. The maple, celandine, columbine, bryony and water crow's foot, which all have healing properties as old herbals testify, may be carved on the shrine to remind the pilgrims that St Frideswide had learnt the art of healing from her aunt, the Abbess of New Minster. The four heads of crowned queens on the south side, and of two saints on the north, with the heads of Edward III and a bishop at the angles, once brightly coloured but all now badly mutilated, added to the royal magnificence of the shrine.

Oxford possessed other holy places. In the still surviving chapel of St Bartholomew's Hospital just outside the city pilgrims could see such wonders as the comb of St Edmund, the bones of St Stephen, the skin of St Bartholomew, and a rib of St Andrew. The comb of the King and Martyr cured the headaches of those pilgrims who passed it through their hair. Thus relics would be used for medical treatment in early hospitals. At the hospital's greater namesake in London, founded in 1123 by a favourite courtier of Henry I as a result of a vow made while he lay sick in Rome, the founder Rahere treated a woman with a grossly swollen tongue thus: 'revolving his relics that he had of the Cross, he dipped them in water and washed the tongue of the patient therewith and with the tree of life, that is with the same sign of the cross upon the same tongue. And in the same hour all the swelling went his way, and the woman glad and whole went home to her own.' Eventually the Fellows of Oriel College secured these treasures of St Bartholomew's Hospital in Oxford for their own church of St Mary in the town.

St Albans *The Protomartyr*

At the beginning of the fourth century Alban lived in the Roman city of Verulamium, close to the junction of two great thoroughfares, the Roman Watling Street and the even more ancient Icknield Way, not twenty-two miles north-west of London. When the Emperor Severus began his persecution of the Christians a priest known later as Amphibalus took refuge in Alban's villa. His long devotions and holy life aroused the interest of Alban, and eventually the fugitive Christian baptized his host into the faith. When Roman soldiers searched the villa they found Alban, who had received a forewarning, dressed in the priest's vestments while Amphibalus scurried through the streets disguised as Alban. Hauled before the magistrate, Alban refused to sacrifice to the gods or disclose where Amphibalus could be found. After a scourging the soldiers led him to the top of the small hill overlooking Verulamium. The legionary appointed to execute him preferred to die beside Alban rather than carry out his orders. Thus the first English Christian martyr (the Protomartyr), dying in 303, like his Master did not lack company in his passion. The soldier who took up and used the fatal sword found that his eyes fell out of his head, or so later medieval legend declares. The Romans eventually caught Amphibalus and executed him too, at Redbourn, four miles away on Watling Street.

The Danes who penetrated this far in the sixth century burnt the first chapel built over the Protomartyr's grave on the hill of his martyrdom. The Venerable Bede had written of this church as a place 'where sick people are healed and frequent miracles take place to this day'. Two centuries later King Offa II of Mercia founded a Benedictine monastery on the site. The Danish menace gave rise to one of the most celebrated controversies over a saint's relics in English history. Apparently the monks of St Alban's Abbey agreed to send their Saint's bones to Ely for safe-keeping; but not trusting their monkish brethren they despatched the skeleton of some anonymous monk, carefully hiding the real remains nearby. After the danger had passed the Ely monks returned the feretory, having removed what they thought were the Saint's relics and substituted for them 'certain adulterine bones'. Abbot Leofric of St Alban's, who had marked his false bones, detected the fraud and yet decided to keep silent. Only when Ely invited pilgrims to come to the shrine of the 'real' St Alban did Leofric break silence and explain that the true relics had never left his church. In 1155 Adrian IV, Nicholas Breakspeare, the only Englishman to become pope (who had been born in the town of St Albans, although the abbey refused to admit him as a novice), appointed three bishops to investigate. They found in

The martyrdom of St Alban, from Matthew Paris's life of the Saint, c. *1240. The executioner catches his own eyes while Alban's soul, seen as a dove with halo, flies heavenwards. (Trinity College, Dublin, MS 127 (E.i.40))*

favour of St Alban's. So Matthew Paris tells us, but then he wrote as a monk of St Alban's. When Edward II visited Ely he was still shown the reputed shrine of St Alban: however, when it was opened, on his orders, Alan de Walsingham the Sacrist could only produce a large piece of 'hairy cloth', which he said was the cloak given to St Alban by Amphibalus.

The Normans rebuilt the abbey church soon after the Conquest, making use of Roman bricks from the deserted ruins of Verulamium. In the chapel behind the later reredos there still stands the pedestal of St Alban's shrine, over eight feet high, designed together with the chapel in 1302–08. Although King Henry's men destroyed the shrine itself during the Dissolution of the Monasteries, later restorers pieced together about two thousand fragments of the canopied work and shafts that once supported it. At the backs of some of the ten niches one can still see the Royal Arms, the three leopards of England and the *fleur-de-lis* in vermilion, blue and gold, while scenes from St Alban's life are carved in relief round the top, along with figures of kings, bishops, and angels swinging incense-holders. Fourteen square shafts once surrounded the structure, and three twisted marble pillars – like those of the shrine of Edward the Confessor in Westminster Abbey (pp. 76–77) – probably held large candles. No representation of the

The martyrdom of St Alban as shown on the end of his shrine.

Below: *the relics of St Alban brought to a chapel outside Verulamium by monks, one of whom proclaims 'Here is our master'. Cripples crawl under the reliquary. From a fourteenth-century life of the Saint. (British Library, London, Cotton MS Nero D.1)*

wooden lid which crowned this base has survived, but it probably resembled those at Canterbury and Durham (pp. 70, 144). The hole in the roof immediately above the shrine once held the rope used to raise and lower the protecting cover.

The fifteenth-century timber watching gallery or loft on the north side is a remarkable survival. Two storeys high, it occupies the space between two piers. The custodian on duty could look down on the pilgrims from the top gallery, while his fellow stood by the recessed aumbries or cupboards on the ground floor which held the minor relics. The craftsman who carved the ornaments on the gallery took his subjects from the everyday life of pilgrims: a man mowing barley, a woman milking a cow, and even a cat with a rat in its mouth. Just north of the watching gallery stands the reconstructed shrine of St Amphibalus.

Having prayed and made their offerings, the pilgrims would go out to drink the waters of St Alban's Well, which the Saint had miraculously called into being in order to slake his thirst on the way to martyrdom. The steep street named Holywell leading down the hill to the ruins of Verulamium perpetuates the memory of this sacred spring. A fourteenth-century pilgrims' hostel stands on the left, a hundred yards down from the abbey. We can imagine the whole street crammed with pilgrims on 21–22 June, the vigil and feast day of the Saint.

Few records of the pilgrims have survived, but Sir Thomas More describes an incident at the shrine which suggests the impact of a new critical spirit, born of wider learning, upon pilgrimage in the early fifteenth century. Humphrey, Duke of Gloucester, brother of Henry V, cared much for learning: he gave his collection of books, including tomes looted from the Louvre, to Oxford University, where they are housed in the magnificent Duke Humphrey's Library in the Bodleian. Seeing a man who claimed to have been blind from birth being led away from the shrine of St Alban by his wife, apparently miraculously cured, the Duke asked him to name the colour of his gown and then those of other bystanders. As the man named them correctly, although he could never have seen these colours before if his story had been true, the Duke ordered him to be committed to the stocks for fraud. The Duke's splendid tomb lies in the south-eastern bay of the chapel of the Protomartyr.

In their watching gallery the custodians of the shrine kept watch night and day upon the treasures these pilgrims left behind them. For once gold, silver and jewels glittered around the bier containing Alban's bones that stood on the lofty pedestal. An antique Roman cameo, so large that a man could not get his hand around it, was taken to women in difficult labour, to whom it brought relief. Henry III gave a rich bracelet, rings and fine cloth; Edward I bequeathed a silver-gilt image of himself; and Edward III bestowed some magnificent jewels. Richard III offered a necklace of gems to the statue of the Virgin Mary which stood at the west end of Alban's tomb. Adam Paulyn gave a silver bowl which was suspended before the shrine to receive the coins of pilgrims. Abbot John Wheathamsteade paid for the *Life* of St Alban to be translated from Latin into English and hung it on the shrine, for the edification of the literate pilgrims, in company with a painting of the Saint.

As in other monasteries, the Benedictine abbots of St Alban's used these riches as a form of reserve wealth: just as secular lords cashed their gold and silver plate on occasion, twice they sold pilgrims' offerings in order to provide food for the poor after severe famines; on a third occasion they purchased with the money the manor and lands of Brentford. Abbot Simon, the friend of Becket, borrowed heavily to repair the shrine and adorn it with gold, and Aaron, the Jew of Lincoln, could humorously boast that his money had helped buy St Alban a new home. Early in the thirteenth century, short of cash again, this time for the new west front of the church (not the present one, which dates from the nineteenth century), the monks carried the reliquary on shoulder poles around the countryside, accompanied by a man whom the Protomartyr had raised from the dead, a procession which 'heaped together no small sum of money' towards the rebuilding costs.

St Albans: the shrine and, behind it, the watching loft. On the right is a twisted marble shaft which probably formed part of a tall candlestick.

The lower stage of the watching gallery of the shrine, facing outwards to the aisle. The carvings at the top include a seated woman, a cat carrying a rat, a shepherd playing pipes, two wrestlers and a fantastic lion.

Opposite: *the nave of St Albans Cathedral, originally the abbey church. Eleventh-century Norman piers are decorated with thirteenth- and fourteenth-century paintings, including a figure of St Thomas of Canterbury on the front of the pier in the foreground.*

Lichfield *St Chad*

St Chad, a Celtic saint who died in 672, spent his life as a missionary in the Saxon kingdom of Mercia. Even after becoming the first Bishop of Lichfield in 669 he continued to wander around his vast diocese, preaching and baptizing the inhabitants. The numerous wells named after him in the bounds of Mercia and beyond are testimony of his restless Celtic travels. At Lichfield itself Chad prayed in an oratory beside his well, and on winter days stood naked in the cold water to mortify his flesh. The well still exists in a small garden next to St Chad's Church. At one time church leaders and flocks of children visited it on Maundy Thursday and dressed it with boughs and flowers, an ancient pagan custom baptized into Christianity which continues in some places, notably at Tissington in Derbyshire.

Chad's remains rested first in a plain wooden shrine in the churchyard of St Mary's at Lichfield. Bede described it as 'a wooden monument, made like a little house covered, having a hole in the wall, through which those that go thither for devotion usually put in their hand and take out some of the dust, which they put into water and give to sick cattle or men to taste, upon which they are presently eased of their infirmity and restored to health'. When Bishop Walter Langton completed the rebuilding of the cathedral of St Peter with the splendid Lady Chapel early in the fourteenth century he installed there a new shrine, at the enormous cost in those days of two thousand pounds. After the Dissolution various people preserved and passed down the relics of the Saint, and some of his bones are believed to lie today in the Roman Catholic Cathedral at Birmingham, built by the great Gothic Revival architect A. W. N. Pugin in 1839–41, which is dedicated to St Chad.

At some stage the separated head of the Saint, placed in a head reliquary, stood in the Chapel of the Head of St Chad, south of the choir in Lichfield Cathedral. From the Sacrist's Roll it is clear that this painted wooden *chef* lived in an iron-bound coffer enclosed in another chest. In the chapel today the visitor can still see an aumbry used for storing relics. A fourteenth-century stone gallery separates the chapel from the south choir aisle.

The Hands Well at Tissington, dressed for Ascension Day – a ceremony said to date back to the Black Death.

Opposite: *gallery in Lichfield Cathedral from where the reliquary containing the head of St Chad may have been shown to pilgrims. The Chapel of St Chad's Head lies beyond it.*

Worcester *St Oswald and St Wulfstan*

Saxon bishops had their seat at Worcester from the seventh century, but little is known about the church there until 964, when Bishop (later Saint) Oswald founded a Benedictine monastery. After the Danes had burnt it in 1041, Bishop Wulfstan began to rebuild it on a much larger scale. Fire again ravaged his cathedral, but a successor, Bishop Sylvester, built a new cathedral and in 1218 before the eyes of King Henry III he removed the relics of St Wulfstan, as the Bishop had become, to a new shrine. A favoured guest, the Abbot of St Alban's, took home with him one of the Saint's ribs, which he enclosed in a gold reliquary and placed on an altar dedicated to St Wulfstan.

Not much is known about either St Oswald or St Wulfstan. St Oswald died in 992. Aldulf, his successor in the sees of both Worcester and York, moved his bones from their humble tomb and sent most of them to York. During the war between Stephen and Matilda, when a mob sacked Worcester, the monks bore away St Oswald's relics just as the rabble poured in through the monastery gate. Wulfstan, who died in about 1095, was at that time the oldest surviving Saxon bishop – and the only one not replaced by the Norman conquerors. Rome canonized him in 1113.

Below: *the tomb of King John.* Opposite: *part of the one surviving wall of the Guesten Hall, seen from inside, with the cathedral in the background. In this vast hall pilgrims and guests were fed.*

The two shrines achieved wide renown in the Middle Ages. William II presented gold and silver ornaments. In 1207 King John visited Worcester as a pilgrim in great state. When in 1216 the citizens supported the Dauphin Louis against him his soldiers punished them and extorted such a large fine from the priory that the Abbot had to melt down the treasures to pay them. Nevertheless, when he died at Newark some months later King John willed that his body should be entombed in Worcester Cathedral, between the shrines of Oswald and Wulfstan, so that they could assist his journey through purgatory. The two saints are depicted on either side of the head of the King's effigy.

A thirteenth-century manuscript record kept at Worcester entitled *Miracles of St Wulfstan* gives us some vivid glimpses of the methods used to exorcize demons at the shrine. In order to make the sufferers' bodies too uncomfortable a habitation, the exorcists rained blows on a shrieking mad woman and scourged a potter who had gone out of his mind, tying him to an altar and inviting pilgrims to help them. The treatment sometimes worked: a healed boy claimed he saw a reluctant demon leaving his body and shaking its fist at St Wulfstan's relics.

Some medieval people greeted such stories with scepticism. Nicholas of Chin merely laughed when he was invited to go to Worcester in order to see miracles at the shrine. At least one parish priest in the diocese preferred to treat his parishioners with herbs and blood-letting rather than send them to St Wulfstan. The chronicler assured his readers, however, that this physician was 'quite unlike other men'. Perhaps to confound such critics, the Bishop made careful investigations. In general, as the standard of inquiry into miracles grew more rigorous, so their numbers correspondingly declined.

Near the chapter-house at Worcester stand the ruins of the Guesten Hall, the *hospitium* built in 1320 for the pilgrims resorting to St Wulfstan.

Two other bishops of Worcester had become saints, St Dunstan and St Egwin. The shrine of St Egwin lay in the abbey church at Evesham, which he had founded, on a pedestal known as the 'Throne'. This seems to have been a not uncommon name for the lower part of all shrines, which supported chests of relics; it vividly suggests the vision in the medieval imagination of the saints sitting on their rich thrones dispensing their royal favours of healing and forgiveness.

Hereford *St Ethelbert and St Thomas Cantilupe*

Late in the seventh century the great Midlands diocese of Lichfield was subdivided, and the bishopric of Hereford appeared on the ecclesiastical map. In 792 Offa, King of Mercia, who lived at Sutton Walls near Hereford, gave it a saint when he abruptly beheaded Ethelbert, King of the East Angles, the suitor for the hand of his daughter Alfrida. A pillar of light marked Ethelbert's grave at Marden on the night of his burial, and the slain King appeared to his friend Brithfrid during the three following nights asking for his corpse to be removed to the monastery at Hereford. At his second grave miracles abounded. Struck by remorse, Offa ordered the construction of a tomb and church, which eventually grew into the Saxon cathedral of St Mary and St Ethelbert.

By 1275, when Thomas Cantilupe became bishop, this church had been almost completely rebuilt and appeared much as it does today. Thomas had been chancellor of England for the rebel Simon de Montfort, but after Simon's death at the battle of Evesham he relinquished the post. A man greatly respected for his piety and learning, he proved to be also an outstanding pastor. He died of fever in 1282 at Monte Fiascone, near Florence, on his way to Rome to seek the Pope's intervention in his quarrel with the Archbishop of Canterbury. His chaplain Richard Swinfield, anxious to carry his bones back to Hereford, boiled the corpse to separate flesh from skeleton, and preserved the heart in a case – the usual treatment for those, such as crusaders, who died abroad. He buried the flesh in the monastery of S. Severo, near Orvieto.

Above and opposite: *the surviving pedestal of St Thomas Cantilupe's shrine. Offerings made here paid for the building of the central tower of Hereford Cathedral.*

Limoges enamel reliquary depicting the martyrdom of St Thomas Becket, in the Treasury of Hereford Cathedral.

With elaborate ceremony Bishop Richard, for so he had become, and the monks of Hereford installed the bones of Thomas Cantilupe in the Lady Chapel in 1287. His canonization in 1320, the last canonization of an Englishman before the Reformation, recognized the many miracles that took place at his tomb. It is said that Edward I, whose adviser Thomas had been, sent there a wax model of his favourite hunting falcon, which ailed in its cage, together with a handsome purse of coins.

Part of the shrine can still be seen, standing now in the north transept (a remarkable work by Thomas's predecessor, Bishop Aquablanca, and contemporary with the Angel Choir at Lincoln Cathedral). It is the Purbeck marble base which once held the reliquary. The lower part, in the shape of an oblong tomb, is ornamented with fourteen figures of Knights Templar, the order which Thomas served as Provincial Grand Master. A gleaming brass of the Bishop in his mitre and robes once filled the empty matrix on the top of this chest. Above is a canopy resting on arcades with delicate naturalistic leaf-carving which would almost certainly have supported the hut-shaped reliquary box. In 1349 the monks carried the relics on their shoulders around the streets of Hereford to stem the tide of the Black Death.

An early thirteenth-century reliquary of Limoges enamel in the Treasury of Hereford Cathedral is decorated with scenes of the martyrdom and entombment of St Thomas of Canterbury. Imported from France, it probably held one of the many relics of that saint, and served to attract pilgrims to Hereford before that city acquired its own St Thomas.

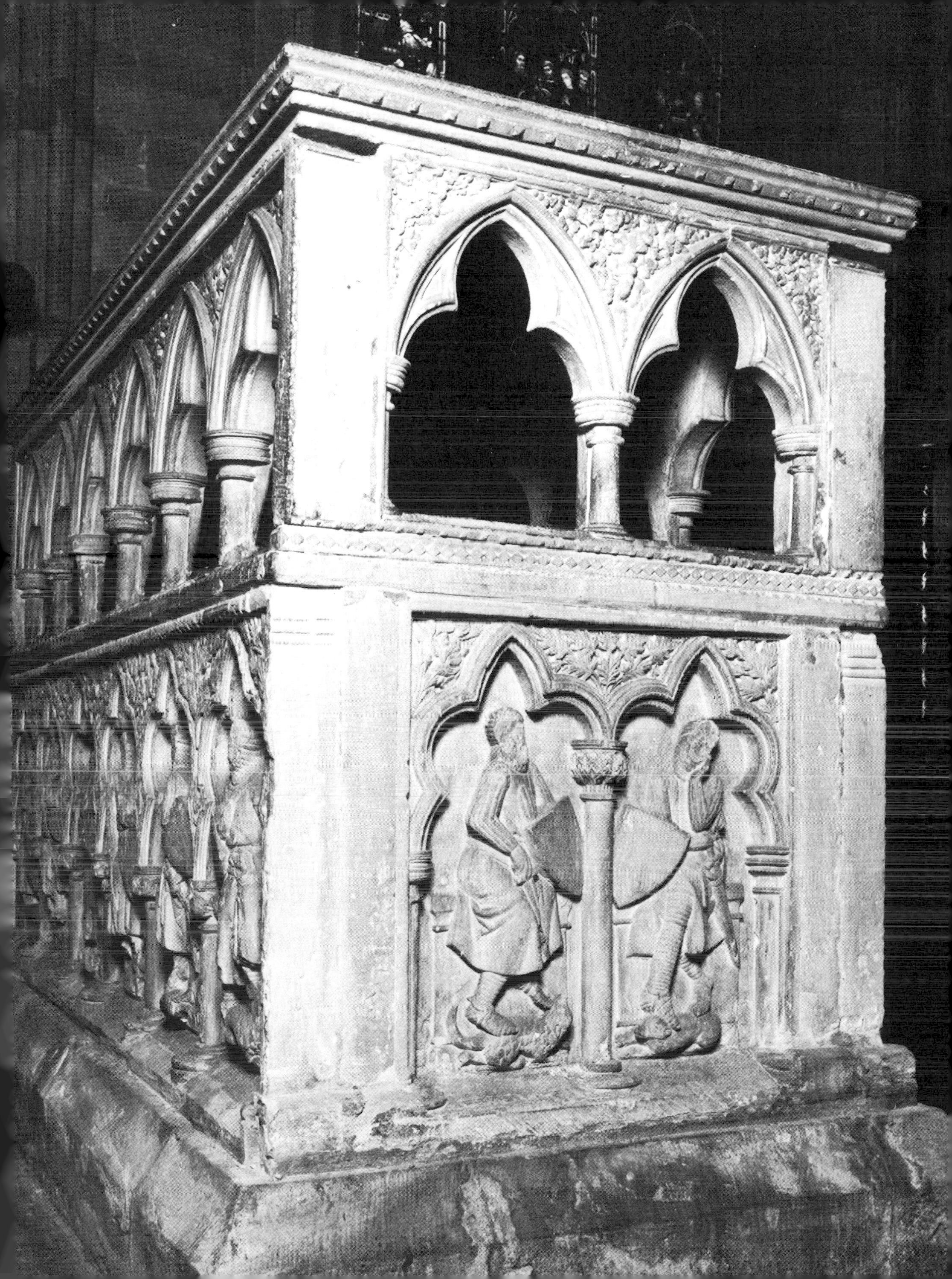

Lincoln *St Hugh of Avalon and Little St Hugh*

Lincoln Cathedral stands on a hill which was already inhabited in prehistoric times. Tradition says that St Paulinus, the missionary bishop of York, converted the Saxon inhabitants in the seventh century. William the Conqueror built the castle, and twenty years after the Conquest the first stones of the Norman cathedral were laid.

In 1186 the chapter elected as bishop a man who was to prove a great churchman and a great saint. Hugh was born about 1135 at Avalon in France, and became a monk at the Grande Chartreuse. In a move typical of the internationalism of the early Middle Ages, he was brought to England by Henry II – Becket's king – to be prior of the recently founded Charterhouse of Witham in Somerset, and then, again with Henry's support, placed in charge of the vast diocese of Lincoln. He remained attached to that austere and solitary order, but he was a man of action; we know his deeds and character from the remarkable *Life* written by his friend the monk Adam. He was 'peppery' and 'fearless as a lion': twice, at Lincoln and Northampton, he stood up alone to anti-Jewish mobs. Yet he could be gentle and winning, and his emblem is his pet tame swan.

He travelled widely: one story in the *Life* seems almost out of keeping with his character, but it exemplifies the avidity for holy relics which consumed even the best men. While staying as a guest at the abbey of Fécamp in Normandy he was shown the arm of St Mary Magdalen, bound tightly in bandages. Despite his hosts' angry protests, Hugh drew out a knife, sliced open the cloth and tried to break off a finger from the arm. Finally, biting 'first with his incisors and finally with his molars', he chewed away two pieces of finger which he gave into the custody of his monk biographer. 'If a little while ago I handled the sacred body of the Lord with my fingers in spite of my unworthiness and partook of it with my lips and teeth,' he explained to the Abbot, 'why should I not treat the bones of the saints in the same way . . . and without profanity acquire them wherever I can?' With this spirit abroad it is not surprising that monks and clergy stood watch over their relics.

A year before Hugh reached Lincoln a severe earthquake, felt throughout England, cleft the cathedral 'from top to bottom', and it was left to him to begin the work of rebuilding. We know the name of his architect, Geoffrey de Noiers. The new east end which they built is one of the earliest pure Gothic designs in England, and one of the most idiosyncratic. When Hugh lay dying in London in 1200 he charged Geoffrey to make ready an altar in the north-eastern transept 'for a gathering at which he would be present' – his funeral – and there he was buried.

So many pilgrims sought the blessings of St Hugh after his canonization in 1220 that an enlargement of the cathedral was needed, and, thanks largely to their offerings, could be afforded. (Further revenue came from a separate pilgrimage station set up for the Saint's head.) Part of that east end which, we are told, Hugh had helped to build with his own hands was taken down and replaced by the glorious Angel Choir. In 1280 the Saint's remains were translated to the chapel behind the high altar, in the presence of King Edward I. To complete the lavish festivities, two conduits in Lincoln ran red with wine.

No trace remains of St Hugh's principal shrine, destroyed in 1542, but at the easternmost end of the Angel Choir there stands an elegant mid-fourteenth-century structure which was almost certainly the pedestal for his head reliquary. It has two niches on the north side and one in the front; instruments of the Passion adorn the shields over the arches, and the paving-stones before it are much worn. In the fourteenth century thieves stole the golden, gem-encrusted reliquary, but left the skull, probably in its wooden case, in a nearby meadow. A black crow stood guard over the relic until the monks arrived to carry it home. A new setting was fashioned, crowned by an 'orient saphir'.

Pilgrims would also have seen the marble shrine-base and silver reliquary of John of Dalderby, an uncanonized fourteenth-century bishop of Lincoln, whose resting-place in the south transept was signposted by the great rose-window known as the Bishop's Eye. Bishop Grosseteste, builder of the cathedral transepts and nave, was also revered as a saint. Finally, in the south choir aisle pilgrims would have honoured 'Little St Hugh', a child who died in 1255 reputedly crucified by Jews and thrown down a well. In fact the citizens of Lincoln had found his body drowned in the cesspool of a Jew's house, and blinded by anti-semitic feeling inferred the rest. In 1790 a stone coffin was found under his shrine containing a boy's skeleton.

Little St Hugh and St William of Norwich are examples of the trumped-up stories of 'ritual murders' of Christian boys by Jewish communities which were common throughout Europe in the Middle Ages and even later. These fictions cost many innocent Jews their lives. The cathedral authorities at Lincoln have affixed a notice to the shrine of Little St Hugh which concludes: 'Such stories do not redound to the credit of Christendom and so we pray "Remember not, Lord, our offences nor the offences of our forefathers."' Considering Great St Hugh of Avalon's stand against anti-semitism at Lincoln and Northampton, one must find this sharing of names and veneration deeply ironic.

LINCOLN

Previous page: *the Angel Choir, with the stone pedestal of the head shrine of St Hugh in the centre (see p. 139). The original east end of St Hugh's church is traced in outline on the floor.*

Left: *heads of a lion, a monk and a satyr-like creature carved on the pedestal of St Hugh's shrine (seen opposite).*

Below left: *remains of the shrine of Little St Hugh. On the wall above are fragments of its stone canopy.*

Opposite: *pedestal of the head shrine of St Hugh. The reliquary, possibly head-shaped, would have stood on top.*

Derby *St Alkmund*

In the eighth century Alkmund, son of the King of Northumbria, fled northwards with his father when their rebellious subjects concluded a treaty with the Danes. For almost twenty years the pair sojourned in the land of the Picts until a party of young Northumbrian warriors brought news that people had grown weary of the Norsemen and earnestly desired the King and his son to lead their fight for freedom. Alkmund fought at their head against the Danes in several battles. The date and place of his death are not clear from the chroniclers, but he may have been treacherously murdered by the Norsemen in 819. Soon after his death the Northumbrian people hailed him as a martyr and saint; how far he deserved this honour history does not record.

At first St Alkmund lay buried in a church at Lilleshall in Shropshire. Fear of the Danes caused the guardians of his relics to carry them southwards into the Midlands for safety, and they came to rest at Derby on 19 March. The townsfolk adopted him as their saint, keeping that day with great devotion. As Derby lay astride the Roman road of Rykneld Street, one of the main north-south highways of the Middle Ages, the shrine of St Alkmund in the church built over it did not lack pilgrims. Indeed, the fame of the shrine lasted even beyond its destruction by the Tudor reformers. In 1740 the Vicar of St Alkmund's Church could inform a correspondent: 'Fuller in his *Worthies* reports of miracles here, I add that the north countrymen inquire for this tomb, and set their packs upon it.'

The old church of St Alkmund disappeared under the hands of Victorian church-builders, and its successor has disappeared under the hands of modern road-builders. A few ancient crosses are deposited in the local museum, and also a remarkable stone sarcophagus, decorated with a bold Anglo-Saxon interlace pattern, which was found during a rescue 'dig' when the church was demolished and is thought to have been the coffin of St Alkmund himself. The Well of St Alkmund, formerly to the north of the church, used to be decorated with flowers on the Saint's day.

Not far from the site of the old church are the remains of the chapel of St Mary-on-the-Bridge, one of the five bridge chapels which have survived in England. A squint pierced the north wall so that travellers crossing the river could see the Blessed Sacrament. It sadly lost its bridge in favour of a new Georgian one in 1788.

While in the area of Derby it is worth travelling south a dozen miles to Ashby-de-la-Zouch to see the effigy of a late fifteenth-century pilgrim, thought to be Thomas, brother of Lord Hastings. He is shown wearing a long cloak; a narrow strap over his right shoulder carries his scrip or wallet, and he holds a pilgrim's staff. The cockle shells on his broad hat show that he had visited the shrine of St James in Spain.

Sarcophagus thought to be that of St Alkmund. Of the lid only a corner survives. (Derby Museums and Art Gallery)

Opposite: *pilgrim's tomb in St Helen's Church, Ashby-de-la-Zouch.*

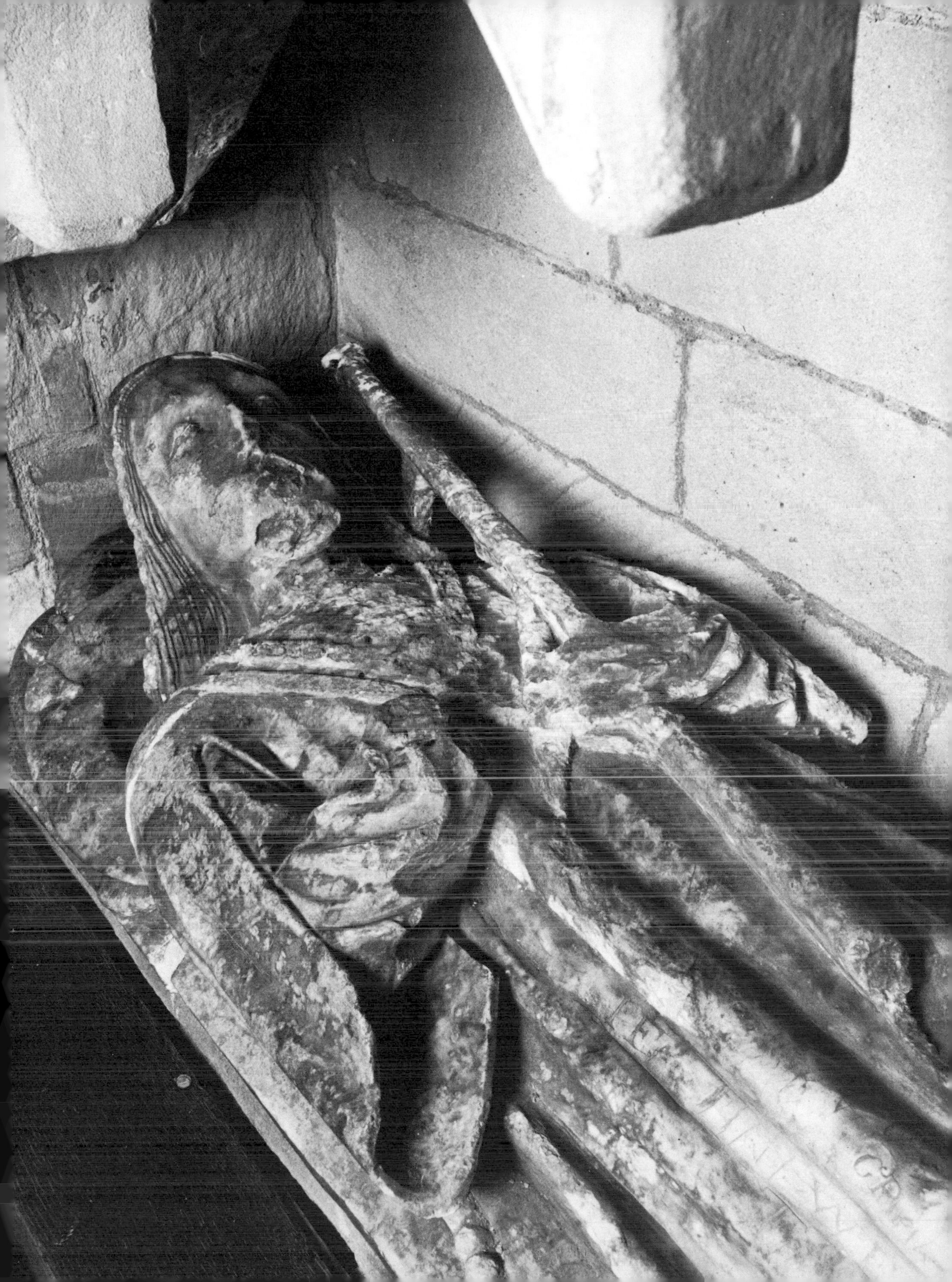

The North

Lindisfarne and Durham *St Cuthbert*

In response to a request from King Oswald of Northumbria for a bishop to convert his pagan subjects to the Christian faith, the monks of Iona sent him first one who proved to be a failure, and then a great saint – Aidan. The new bishop chose another island in 635 as the place for his seat, Lindisfarne. This island possessed three advantages: it lay within sight of Oswald's royal castle of Bamburgh; the sea formed a natural moat around it, ebbing away twice a day to reveal a causeway; and a small rock-girt haven could shelter the largest ships of the day. Here Aidan established his base, a small Celtic monastery. With the King, who even acted in early days as interpreter to the Gaelic-speaking monk, Aidan travelled about the kingdom proclaiming the gospel under easily-erected wooden preaching crosses. One Easter, when they dined together, the King impulsively picked up the silver vessel containing the main dish and gave it away to the poor who crowded at his gates. Aidan touched the King's right hand and said 'May this hand never perish!' A hundred years later, Bede reported that the incorrupt hand and arm of St Oswald – as the King had become – lay in a silver reliquary in St Peter's Church in Bamburgh Castle, much venerated by pilgrims.

On the night of 31 August 651, when Aidan died in the parish church at Bamburgh, a young fair-haired shepherd called Cuthbert stood watching his sheep on the lower slopes of the Lammermuir Hills when he saw a vision of angels soaring upwards bearing a shining great soul. Hearing of Aidan's death some days later he interpreted the vision as a divine vocation to serve God. He left his Christian foster-mother Kenswith, and rode to Melrose Abbey where he joined the community. In those days it occupied a site in the thick forest beside the Tweed, some three miles east of the present abbey.

For thirteen years Cuthbert travelled about the lands north of the Roman Wall, preaching in Gaelic to the people. The county name of Kirkcudbrightshire commemorates him – the church of Cuthbert. While staying with St Ebba he made his way unnoticed save by a prying monk down the cliffs to the sea where he recited Psalms standing waist-deep amid the icy breakers. The monk then saw two young seals or otters come up to him on the beach and dry his feet with their fur. This sympathy of animals for Cuthbert occurs in other stories about him. On one occasion an eagle caught a salmon in the River Teviot and dropped it into the Saint's boat; on another, his horse pulled away some thatch in the hut where he sheltered and revealed bread and meat wrapped up in a cloth. On both occasions Cuthbert characteristically shared his meal with the provider.

Eata, the founder of Melrose, took Cuthbert with him south to be guest-master at the new monastery of Ripon, in an area already influenced by the missionaries of St Augustine after the fall of Mercia (655). Eata would not accept the Roman method of calculating the date of Easter or their style of haircut for monks and priests (the circular tonsure), and so he returned to Melrose, accompanied by his 'affable and pleasant' guest-master, now thirty years old. In 663/64 King Oswy, weary of the confusion – caused not least by his own Celtic observation of Easter at a time when his Kentish Queen still fasted in the Roman Lent – called the Synod of Whitby to resolve the churchmen's differences. Wilfred, from Ripon, argued powerfully in favour of the Latin practices, and the King gave judgment in their favour. Henceforth England was to follow the Roman way of St Augustine rather than the Celtic way of St Columba. Colman of Lindisfarne, together with most of the Scots and a few English monks, refused to accept the verdict and withdrew to Iona bearing with them some of St Aidan's bones. But Bishop Cedd, the interpreter at the Synod, Eata and Cuthbert himself fell in with the decision. Eata became Bishop of Lindisfarne in place of Colman, and appointed Cuthbert as his prior.

For twelve years Cuthbert worked as a leader of the community and also as a missionary on the mainland. But the solitary spirit of the Celtic tradition began to

Opposite: *Bamburgh Castle.* Below: *St Cuthbert praying naked in the sea, and having his feet dried by sea-creatures. From a twelfth-century manuscript of Bede's* Life of St Cuthbert. *(University College, Oxford, MS 165)*

assert itself. He spent long days alone on an adjacent islet known today as St Cuthbert's Island: the foundations of a small oratory can still be seen there. Yet it lay only a stone's throw from Lindisfarne, with its quarrelsome community and the needy or curious visitors desiring to meet him. At the age of about forty-two Cuthbert received permission to retire as prior and to withdraw as a hermit to the uninhabited island of Farne, where Aidan had lived before him. For nine years he lived there in a turf oratory, sunken and walled so that no vista of sea or land could draw his gaze away from heaven. The monks who came to wash his feet on Maundy Thursday were sure that he had not removed his leather boots all year. After several years he did not even open the window of his cell except to bless the pilgrims who rowed themselves across from Bamburgh to seek his intercessions. At first, however, he walked his island and befriended the seals and birds who visited its shores. Many of the eider-ducks allowed him to stroke them as they sat upon their eggs; afterwards local people nick-named them St Cuthbert's Ducks. It is a happy fact that Farne Island is today a bird sanctuary.

Eventually, Cuthbert reluctantly allowed himself to be consecrated bishop and briefly resumed his missionary travels. Folklore has passed down not only the memory of his spiritual gifts of insight and prophecy, sympathy and holiness, but also the odd fact about him, for example that he was left-handed. In 686, sensing the approach of death, he spent the Christmas Feast with the monks of Lindisfarne and then withdrew once more to Farne Island. During his two remaining months of life the monks rowed Abbot Herefrith across to minister to him. Once when storms raged he survived for five days eating just one onion a day. A brother who touched the dying Saint found himself cured of dysentery. On 20 March 687, having received the last Sacrament, Cuthbert looked up to heaven, stretched out his arms and died.

Although he had wished to be buried on Farne Island, Cuthbert allowed the monks to persuade him to will his remains to Lindisfarne on condition that if they were ever compelled to forsake their home they should carry his bones with them, so that he should never rest but among Christians. Dressed in vestments and wrapped in a waxed linen shroud presented by the Abbess Verca of South Shields, Cuthbert's body was solemnly interred in a stone tomb to the right of the altar in the abbey church of Lindisfarne. After eleven years the monks moved the relics to a shrine above ground level so that the pilgrims who thronged across the causeway, known then as the Pilgrims' Way, could touch the coffin.

In 875, when the Danes descended on the coast sacking and pillaging towns and monasteries alike, the 'congregation of St Cuthbert' at Lindisfarne took the coffin of St Cuthbert out of the shrine, opened it up and added to its contents the remaining bones of St Aidan and the head of St Oswald. Bearing these relics in a wooden coffer, together with other treasures offered at the shrine such as the *Lindisfarne Gospels* (said to have been written by Eadfrith, second bishop after Cuthbert), they wandered about Northumbria and Galloway for eight years before settling down at Chester-le-Street. For one hundred and twelve years the Saint's relics and his former see remained based there. But the Danes drove the successors of the Lindisfarne community further south, to Durham, where in 995 these monks built a 'little church of wands and branches' to shelter the relics upon the rocky plateau in a loop of the River Wear where the massive Norman cathedral now stands.

In 1091 the second Norman bishop of Durham, William of St Carileph, laid the foundations of a great abbey church for the Benedictine order and the bones of St Cuthbert were translated into the incomplete building in 1104. The whole structure, finished in 1133, retains its massive Norman character today despite later additions and modifications, half house of God, half castle 'gainst the Scots'. Prior Melsanby added in 1242 the Chapel of the Nine Altars beyond the high altar and the bones of St Cuthbert were subsequently translated into a famous shrine at its entrance. The *Rites of Durham* tell us that the shrine was

> exalted with the most curious workmanship, of fine and costly green marble, all limned [painted] and gilt with gold; having four seats or places, convenient underneath the shrine, for the pilgrims or lame men, setting on their knees to lean and rest on, in the time of their devout offerings and fervent prayers to God and Holy St Cuthbert, for his miraculous relief and succour, which being never wanting, made the shrine to be so richly invested that it was esteemed one of the most sumptuous monuments in all England . . .
>
> The cover of the shrine being wainscot . . . to which six very fine sounding bells were fastened which stirred all men's hearts, that were in the church to repair unto it. On either side of the said cover were painted four lively images, curiously wrought and miraculous to all beholders thereof. Also within the feretory . . . were almeries [recesses], varnished and finely painted and gilt over with fine little images, for the relics belonging to St Cuthbert to lie in; all the costly reliques and jewels that hung about within the said feretory upon the irons being accounted the most sumptuous and rich jewels in the land.

The Vice-Prior of the Benedictine abbey served as Keeper of the Feretory. He stood by while his clerk drew up the heavy cover of the shrine by a system of ropes and pulleys.

> It was ever drawn in the matins time, or at evensong, when the *Magnificat* was sung. And when they had made their

Monks praying at St Cuthbert's shrine. From a twelfth-century manuscript of Bede's life of the Saint. (University College, Oxford, MS 165)

> prayers and did offer anything to it, if it were either gold, silver or jewels, straightway it was hung on the shrine. And if it were any other thing, as unicorn horn, elephant tooth, or suchlike thing, then it was hung within the feretory, at the end of the shrine. And when the pilgrims had made their prayers the clerk did let down the cover thereof, and did look every corner, giving the keys to the Vice-Prior again.

In other words, as at Canterbury, the shrine acted as a safe for the monastery.

The annual Feast of St Cuthbert attracted thousands of pilgrims. In 1347 the Durham cellarer fed the monks and poorer pilgrims during the week-long festivities with 600 salt-herrings, 400 white herrings, 30 salted salmon, 12 fresh salmon, 14 ling, 4 turbot, 2 horse-loads of white fish, 9 oxen, 7½ pigs, 14 calves, 3 kids, 26 suckling pigs, 71 geese, 14 capons, 59 chickens, 60 pigeons, 5 stone of hog's lard, 4 stone of cheese and butter, 2 quarts of vinegar, 2 quarts of honey, 14 pounds of figs and raisins, and 1300 eggs. The pilgrims would be men, for St Cuthbert's bones (like their owner) seem to have disliked women. At Lindisfarne he had a separate chapel built for their use. At Durham the monks would not allow women near his shrine, and a dark line near the west end of the nave of the cathedral marks the boundary they could not cross.

Throughout the Middle Ages the miraculous powers of the relics grew in fame. St Cuthbert's banner, made from a part of his shroud, helped to bring victory to the English at Flodden. Grateful or hopeful pilgrims adorned the shrine with their gifts – a lance of wax from a pilgrim healed of a lance wound, a girdle of green silk laced with silver, two pairs of pillows, 'one of Cuthbert downe, his eider duck'. To some extent the custodians of the shrine saw themselves in competition with each other. In 1171, within a year of Becket's death, a sick Norwegian cast lots three times to see if he should go to the shrines of Cuthbert, Edward or Thomas. The lots directed him to Durham where the Saint healed him. Later a Berwick boy with acute dysentery who paused at Durham on his way south to Canterbury found St Cuthbert well able to cure him.

Today the bones of St Cuthbert and the head of St Oswald lie under a grey stone slab inscribed simply CUTHBERTUS.

Pilgrims would also have visited the shrine of the famous scholar and biographer of Cuthbert, the Venerable Bede. It once stood encased in gold and silver in the twelfth-century Galilee Chapel at the west end of the cathedral. Now Bede's bones lie beneath a plain table tomb in the same place. Author of the great *Ecclesiastical History of England*, Bede lived for most of his life as a monk at Monkwearmouth and Jarrow. When Cuthbert died he was fourteen years old, and thus he compiled his biography of the Saint from the evidence of those who knew Cuthbert personally.

The tomb of the Venerable Bede.

(Indeed, if historians of the British Isles feel the need of a patron saint they could do no better than choose Bede.) He did not receive the posthumous title of 'Venerable' for over a century. According to legend the monk charged with writing the inscription became stuck for a word to complete his couplet:

Hac sunt in fossa
Bedae ossa.

That night an angelic hand filled in the missing word *Venerabilis*.

Some of the relics which were removed from the shrine of St Cuthbert in 1827 can now be seen in the great medieval dormitory of the abbey. The Saint's pectoral cross, made of gold and set with garnets of deep transparent red, escaped the attention of the Reformation despoilers because it lay hidden in folds of cloth against his breastbone. His portable wooden altar, plated with silver after his death, bears five consecration crosses on its surface. A large plain double-sided ivory comb also found in the coffin was probably St Cuthbert's liturgical comb (used in the early Middle Ages during the celebration of the Mass), and it may also have been used by Ealdrid the Sacrist, who was guardian of the shrine in the eleventh century, for he is said to have cared for the incorrupt body of St Cuthbert, taking pains to trim 'the ever-growing hair of his venerable head' and to 'cut his nails with a pair of silver scissors which he had made'.

Left and below: *St Cuthbert's stole, showing the prophet Amos, and his pectoral cross.* Opposite: *Lindisfarne, looking from the twelfth-century priory church across the anchorage to the castle.*

Among the various embroideries, braids, woven silks and other textile fragments the searchers found a stole with its companion maniple. They are among the oldest surviving pieces of English embroidery: an inscription proclaims that they were made for a bishop of Winchester who ruled shortly after 900. King Athelstan may have presented them to the Saint's shrine when he paused at Chester-le-Street in 934 on his way north to meet the Scottish King, for his list of offerings mentioned a 'girdle'. From documentary evidence it is clear that a small chalice and paten, silver scissors and a gold pastoral staff once accompanied these relics but disappeared at the time of the Dissolution of the Monasteries. Even so, the existing objects form the most remarkable collection of relics in the British Isles.

St Cuthbert's tomb in Durham Cathedral. His shrine stood on this raised platform, with the back of the high altar reredos to the west (right) and the Chapel of the Nine Altars to the east, reached by steps on the north and south.

Durham Cathedral, looking east from the nave. St Cuthbert's tomb lies behind the delicate white stone reredos in the distance – the Neville Screen, presented in 1380. Women could go no nearer the shrine than our viewpoint here.

Ripon and Hexham *St Wilfred*

Born in 634, Wilfred began his education at the royal court of Northumbria. After ordination he studied in Rome, and on his return he enjoyed the favour of the son of Oswiu, King of Northumbria. The monastery at Ripon, founded earlier in the century by Irish-trained monks from Melrose and Iona, passed into his care. At the Synod of Whitby in 664 Wilfred supported the Roman tradition (see p. 143). After the triumph of papal authority and the associated Latin customs, he was consecrated a bishop in Gaul.

While Wilfred sojourned in Gaul another future saint, Chad, became Bishop of Lindisfarne. After his return Wilfred lived for some time at Ripon until Chad resigned in his favour in 669. Wilfred chose York as the centre of his Northumbrian diocese. Nine years later the Northumbrian King quarrelled violently with him and sent him on his travels again. Having preached the gospel to the heathen Frieslanders, Wilfred resorted to Rome to plead his case, but the Northumbrians merely ignored the papal decree in his favour which he had obtained. A man of tireless energy, he occupied his exile in a missionary visit to the South Saxons in what is now Sussex. There he founded the monastery of Selsey. Later he was restored to York but after five years his powerful enemies drove him into exile once more. This time he settled in Mercia, and then sailed again for Rome where he secured another papal decree which paved the way for him to become Bishop of Hexham on his return.

Below: *early Anglo-Saxon chalice found at Hexham. Made of gilt copper and less than three inches high, it would have been used with a portable altar.* Opposite: *the crypt of Hexham Abbey. Beyond the first arch is an antechamber; beyond the second, the relic chamber. Notice the distinctive criss-cross tooling of the re-used Roman stones.*

Wilfred died at Oundle, aged seventy-six. The monks of Ripon carried his body to their abbey for burial. It may possibly have rested under the present Ripon Minster in the Saxon crypt where Wilfred had displayed the relics he had brought from Rome. His shrine stood in the north choir aisle.

The spirit of St Wilfred can perhaps be sensed best at Hexham. Here he had built the predecessor of the present abbey church in the days of his episcopate. His master masons began work in 674, bringing stone from the Roman camp at Corstopitum (Corbridge). The crypt designed by them is probably the finest early crypt extant in north-west Europe. It consists of an innermost chamber, where the relics would have been kept, and two antechambers. Pilgrims made their way from the nave down a narrow stair into the first antechamber, from which – no doubt through a grille – they could see the shrine. Then they departed through the other antechamber (upon whose doorway they may have noticed, among the re-used Roman stones, one which had served as an altar to Apollo Maponus), and ascended a stairway to the north-east. A similar stair on the south side of the choir, no doubt for the clergy alone, led directly to the relic chamber. This 'holy of holies' – which according to tradition housed a relic of St Andrew brought from Rome by St Acca, Wilfred's successor at Hexham – was lit by three cresset lamps, small stone bowls set in the walls, which would be filled with oil and the wick set floating in it.

In the much-restored church above some part of the early floor remains, as well as a fifteenth-century rood screen with sixteen painted panels depicting various saints and prelates, and part of a retable, or altar-back, of similar date and subject. The apse at the end of St Wilfred's original church probably curved just beyond the site of the screen in the present choir. His reputed bishop's seat or *cathedra*, known as St Wilfred's Chair or the Frith Stool, may be standing in the same position as it occupied more than twelve centuries ago, facing down into the body of the church. This remarkable low seat, scooped from a single stone and incised with restrained ornamentation, may have been in the centre of the clergy bench around the apse. According to tradition, it served as the coronation throne of the kings of Northumbria, and it was also connected with the privilege of sanctuary (*frith* in Old English means 'peace'), whereby anyone taking refuge in a church could claim freedom from pursuers or the law.

Ripon Cathedral seen across the River Ure.

Opposite: *the choir of Hexham Abbey and the Frith Stool, known also as St Wilfred's Chair, of* c. *681. It stands above the foundations of the apse of the Saxon church.*

Beverley *St John*

An almost exact contemporary of St Wilfred, this kindly and tolerant man from Harpham-on-the-Wolds in East Yorkshire was Bishop of Hexham and then Archbishop of York before retiring to Beverley, where he died in 721. Many pleasing stories about him were handed down. On one occasion, for example, he interrupted his journey to allow the students who accompanied him to hold a horse-race. Horse-racing had a religious significance in the pagan religions which Christianity replaced, and there may be an echo of an ancient heathen custom in the story.

St John possessed considerable medical knowledge according to the lights of his day. The nuns of Watton asked him to heal a girl who lay dangerously ill after being bled. He asked the Abbess when the operation had been carried out, and upon being told that the surgeon had let the blood in the first quarter of the moon he reprimanded her for allowing such a thing, declaring that Theodore of Tarsus, the saintly Archbishop of Canterbury, had taught him in his youth to avoid blood-letting 'when the light of the moon and the tide of the ocean are waxing'.

The Venerable Bede relates that St John built the first minster at Beverley on the site of a much older church. After his death his body lay for a time in St Peter's Chapel, but following his canonization in 1037 the clergy moved him to a gold-plated shrine behind the high altar. The east end of his church was rebuilt after 1230 to provide a grander setting, and the nave followed in the early fourteenth century. St John's shrine finally stood on a glorious triple-arched screen facing east behind the high altar, built in the mid-fourteenth century by the powerful Percys of Northumberland in conjunction with a family tomb. (Today his bones rest at the east end of the nave.)

Below: *the present grave of St John of Beverley in the nave of the Minster, looking towards the west door.*

Opposite: *the arched screen of the shrine, east of the high altar. (The seventeenth-century monument is of course an intruder.) Beyond the screen at the right the top of the richly decorated Percy Tomb can be seen.*

Near the shrine hung the famous banner of St John. In 1137 Archbishop Thurstan bore it to the Battle of the Standard, together with the banners of St Cuthbert, St Peter of York, and St Wilfred of Ripon. One eye-witness saw them 'all suspended from one pole, like the mast of a ship, surmounted by a cross, in the centre of which was fixed a silver casket, containing the consecrated wafer of the Holy Sacrament. The pole was stepped in a four-wheel cart on which the bishop stood.' The consecrated banners so inspired the episcopal leaders and their army that the Scottish invaders soon fled back across the border. Subsequently the banner of St John followed the Scots back to their lair, for the army of Edward I fought under it during his campaigns in Scotland. On the morning of Agincourt holy oil seeped from the Saint's shrine, a sign of support for which Henry V later returned thanks by presenting costly offerings.

Besides these martial interests the Saint, through his relics, exercised a special influence on animals. William of Malmesbury records that bulls would not fight the bull-dogs loosed upon them in the churchyard of Beverley Minster: the proximity of the Saint's bones rendered them gentle as lambs. The waters of St John's Well at Harpham apparently had the same effect on all wild or savage-natured beasts.

York *St William*

Under the Romans Eboracum became a most important military and trading city. Both the Emperors Hadrian and Septimius Severus made it their headquarters when they visited the province in order to secure its northern frontiers. After the departure of the Roman legions York eventually became the capital of the kingdom of Northumbria. One of the bishops in the Romano-British church had had his seat in York, and in 601 St Augustine revived the see when he made Paulinus Bishop of York. Twenty-six years later this ardent missionary baptized King Edwin in a spring of water under a wooden chapel. The majestic cathedral that we see today thus arose over a simple holy well.

York was powerful as the only see besides Canterbury to have an archbishop; yet for all its glories the minster lacked a saint who could draw the pilgrims until 1226, when the Pope canonized William FitzHerbert, a twelfth-century archbishop of York. His relics were rehoused in a tall shrine behind the high altar. Antony Bek, Bishop of Durham from 1283 to 1310 (and afterwards Patriarch of Jerusalem), paid for the translation out of his princely pocket, and attended the ceremony in the presence of Edward III and his queen. Later the east end of the Minster was rebuilt, and in 1471 St Wilfred's relics were translated again, to a structure which was the largest of all the English shrines.

Below: *the tomb of St William. The crypt where his Roman sarcophagus now lies was rebuilt in the nineteenth century, revealing fragments of the ornate Norman pillars.*

Opposite: *York Minster seen from the city wall to the north of it.*

At the time of the Reformation Dr Layton, who became Dean of York, petitioned successfully for the head of St William in its silver *chef*. No one ever saw it again. An antiquary in 1732 dug up the Saint's bones from under a marble slab in the nave where the Tudor reformers had buried them, and found them mingled carelessly together in a leaden box. Fragments of the great shrine, and of the other shrine that stood on the site of the tomb in the nave, are now in the Yorkshire Museum.

No memorials of the many pilgrims who came to the shrine have survived, save a remarkable stone now on view in the crypt. It fell from a great height on the head of a pilgrim, but, as the inscription incised upon it recounts, the fortunate man had a miraculous escape from death. This vivid story is depicted, with many other miracles, in the vast St William stained glass window, erected in 1422–23 in the north-eastern transept.

For all pilgrims the inns and hospices of York possessed smaller hazards far more common than tumbling masonry in the minster. About 1400 an Englishman wrote a textbook on the French language in which he gave some specimens of conversation. A servant sent forward to reserve a bed asks the innkeeper to verify 'that there are no fleas, nor bugs, nor other vermin'. 'No, sir,' replies the host, 'for I make bold that you will be well and comfortably lodged here – save that there is a great peck of rats and mice.' At another hostelry one traveller tells his bed-fellow: 'William, undress and wash your legs, and then dry them with a cloth, and rub them well for love of the fleas, that they may not leap on your legs, for there is a peck of them lying in the dust under the rushes . . . Hi! the fleas bite me so! and do me great harm for I have scratched my shoulders till the blood flows.' Doubtless once the pilgrims set foot inside the glorious minster and hastened to kneel at the shrine of St William, the memory of these nocturnal irritations faded like darkness before the morning light.

Today the Saint's bones lie in a simple shrine in the western part of the crypt, and both Anglican and Roman Catholic services held there help to keep his memory alive.

Detail of the St William Window (1422–23). Reading across from left to right, the panels show: (1) a woman displaying her hand after the ordeal of fire; (2) she kneels at the shrine; (3) a man with his feet in fetters; (4) a man hanging tapestries, preparing for a procession of the feretory; (5) he is knocked from the ladder by a stone; (6) unharmed, he leads the procession carrying the stone; (7) a man offering a wax leg at the shrine; (8) the feretory carried across a collapsing bridge; (9) a boy with contracted joints healed by the feretory; (10) a drowned child, revived, presented at the shrine; (11) a cripple near the relics; (12) a dumb woman, in bed, declares a vision.

Opposite: *the nave of York Minster, looking east towards the late fifteenth-century choir screen. Here stood the popular shrine known as the Tomb of St William, where veneration continued although the Saint's body was buried in the great shrine to the east.*

The Welsh Marches and Wales

Chester *St Werburgh*

Werburgh was born the daughter of King Wulfhere of Mercia, a son of that formidable pagan champion Penda, who recovered his father's kingdom from the Northumbrians in the seventh century. Beyond her reputation for sanctity not much is now known about her, except that she took the veil at a young age and became a renowned abbess. As a sign of her sanctity, like other holy virgins it was rumoured that she could hang her veil on a sunbeam. She was kind to every creature of God, even the wild geese who ravaged her fields at Weedon. On one occasion, it was said, the Saint had driven into her presence a huge flock: after shutting them indoors for a night she pardoned them. When the birds discovered that one of their number was missing – stolen by a servant – they winged their way noisily back to the Saint. Werburgh at once understood the meaning of their cries and secured the release of their fellow. She rejoiced with them, saying 'Birds of the air, bless the Lord!'. The whole flock then flew away, and no bird of that feather was ever found again on the land of the blessed Werburgh. When she died her nuns buried her at Hanbury, where she rested until the Danish threat in 875 forced their successors to bear her relics into the walled city of Chester for safe-keeping.

Henry Lupus, Earl of Chester and Lord of the Welsh Marches, founded the Benedictine abbey of St Werburgh in 1093. Built of red sandstone, it occupied the north-east corner of the medieval city. The monks gradually rebuilt and enlarged their church, adding a fine Lady Chapel in the thirteenth century (where the shrine now stands), and, in the later Middle Ages, a south transept so vast that it served at one time as the parish church. At the eastern end of the north choir aisle a special late Gothic chapel housed St Werburgh's shrine below pretty star vaulting.

In 1186, when a great fire swept through the crowded wooden tenements of the city, the monks trooped in procession around the flames carrying the relics of St Werburgh. Whether they proved as obedient as the wild geese, history does not record.

At the Dissolution the monks' church was made into a cathedral, and the base of the shrine moved and transformed into a base for the bishop's throne. Towards the end of the last century it was carefully reconstructed in its original form of about 1310, with two tiers of richly carved arcading and a host of statuettes representing the Mercian royal family.

The shrine of St Werburgh in Chester Cathedral.

Opposite: *the modern shrine of St David, in a small niche backing on to the high altar in St David's Cathedral (see p. 170). The circular opening above the reliquary box allows glimpses into the choir and nave.*

Holywell *St Winifride's Well*

Above and below: *St Beuno's Chest, and St Beuno's Well, with Clynnog Fawr Church in the background.*

Opposite, above: *St Winifride's shrine in Shrewsbury Church.*

Opposite, below: *St Winifride's Well. George Cuitt's etching of 1813 exaggerates the scale, but shows that the infirm still flocked to the well with its star-shaped back.*

Early in the seventh century, the mountains of North Wales attracted many Celtic saints searching for solitude. One of them, St Beuno, received hospitality in the house of a Welsh chieftain, and instructed the Welshman's daughter Winifride in the mysteries of the Christian religion. Eventually her parents agreed to their daughter's plea that she should enter a convent.

One day, Prince Caradoc, son of King Alan, surprised Winifride alone in the house and threw his arms around her. She slipped away and ran towards St Beuno's church for safety, but he overtook her in Dry Valley; she refused him again, and the enraged Caradoc sliced through her slender white neck with his sword. The stones about bore her bloodstains for evermore, and where her head first touched the ground a healing well burst forth. The blood falling in the water also dyed the moss red, and gave it a sweet odour of frankincense or violets. (There are in fact two species of moss growing there, one of which Linnaeus called the 'violet-smelling'.) According to legend, Winifride's head rolled through the open church door and the congregation rushed out to find the prince standing beside the murdered girl. But St Beuno fastened the severed head on the body, breathed air into her mouth and nostrils, and prayed until she stood up alive and well. Meanwhile the body of Caradoc, who had fallen dead under the Saint's curse, slowly melted away before their eyes.

Some years later, on the evening before he left the region St Beuno took the young woman to the spring and prophesied that those who sought her aid at the wellside should obtain their heart's desire – at the second or third time of asking if not the first. Beuno asked her to send him a cloak woven with her own hands, as an annual gift of gratitude, by placing it in the stream which would bear it miraculously to him wherever he might be. Having blessed her, he took up his staff and continued his wandering life. Each year on May Day she placed a cloak in the stream, which reached him in perfect condition, hence his name in Wales – Beuno of the Dry Cloak. He is said to be buried in a chapel called Eglwys y Bedd ('the Church of the Shrine') at Clynnog Fawr in North Wales, where a stone, money chest and well associated with him by name can still be seen.

One tradition says that St Winifride founded a convent at Holywell, as the spring became known, and lived there after St Beuno died. There is general agreement, however, that she died in the mountains at Gwytherin near the source of the River Elwy. In the twelfth century the religious house at Shrewsbury acquired her relics and her shrine in the monastery church became a popular place of pilgrimage. At the Dissolution the agents of Henry VIII scattered her bones, but one finger survived. From Powis Castle it was sent to Rome, and then returned to England in 1852 and divided between Holywell and Shrewsbury. A piece of the shrine, showing St Winifride with St John the Baptist on her right and St Beuno on her left, stands at the west end of the former abbey church at Shrewsbury.

Today Holywell, which lies on the west side of the Dee estuary about four miles north-west of Flint, shows the finest surviving example in Britain of a medieval holy well. The spring is housed in a two-storeyed structure built about 1500 by Margaret Beaufort, mother of Henry VII. Above is a small chapel projecting out from the steep hillside, while below is the star-shaped well, covered by an ornate vault and surrounded by a processional passage or ambulatory. In the courtyard outside the pilgrim could bathe in a long pool. Just beneath the surface of the water lies the stone upon which St Beuno is said to have stood when he bade farewell to Winifride. In the valley beyond, pilgrims would pause and pray before a number of

A medieval carving at Holywell which suggests that it was the custom, then as now, to carry sick pilgrims down the steps into the water. (These figures can be seen top right in the etching on p. 163.) Opposite: *Looking across the well (from right to left in the etching, p. 163), towards a statue of St Winifride. Below the arch steps lead down to the well; above it, one T. M. Carew of Meath carefully recorded his cure in 1831.*

stones stained by the Saint's blood which was miraculously renewed each year.

Early in the fifteenth century the Pope granted the right to sell special indulgences to all pilgrims visiting Holywell to the abbey of Basingwerk, on the coast about two miles to the north, which acquired the custody of the Well. One of the monks there compiled a list of healing miracles wrought by St Winifride. A house of the Knights Templar stood near the abbey and its occupants protected pilgrims to Holywell from the hazards of robbers and brigands who abounded on those wild roads of North Wales. In 1416 Henry V 'with great reverence went on foot' in pilgrimage to St Winifride's Well.

Under Queen Elizabeth recusant Catholics still made their pilgrimage to the Well, and enjoyed there the services of a priest called Father John Bennet who chose to be racked at Ludlow Castle rather than abjure his faith. Pilgrims still experienced miraculous cures. In 1574 a servant called William Shone so forgot his pious purpose as to wash his boots in the Well. At once he was paralysed, and only by coming back twice a day did he secure the Saint's healing forgiveness. In 1602 Elizabeth Roberts recovered from a stroke and two years later blind Catherine Moore could see again. On 3 November 1629, St Winifride's Day, fifteen hundred people headed by some notable Catholic families made another pilgrimage. Eight years later the justices of the peace at Chester issued orders to their officers to shut all but two of the inns in the town of Holywell. They also whitewashed the Saint's image and removed the iron railings around the pool – possibly in the hope that some pilgrims would drown themselves. Subsequently the justices fined the two hostelers for failing to report to them the names of pilgrims who lodged in their inns. Apparently Catholics bought both the Star Inn and the Cross Keys during that century so that Mass could be said in them.

King James II came in 1686 to the Well, which was staffed (as again now) by the Jesuits, who had renewed their mission in North Wales in 1670. A stone in the basin inscribed 1683 commemorates the restoration of the chapel by his wife Mary of Modena, to whom he had presented it. Two years after James's visit the Protestant supporters of William III ransacked the chapel and drove out the priest-in-charge. Yet when Celia Fiennes visited Holywell in 1698 she saw pilgrims kneeling beside their crutches around the shrine. In the authentic voice of an educated and intellectual Puritan she wrote that they were 'deluded by an ignorant blind zeal and are to be pitied by us that have the advantage of knowing better and ought to be better'.

Dr Samuel Johnson journeyed to the Well in 1774 and thought the bath indecent, for 'a woman bathed while we all looked on'. A century later the newly opened hospice for pilgrims lodged over a thousand guests in its first year. In 1851 and 1887 Popes granted indulgences to pilgrims going to Holywell. Thus it is the only shrine in Britain with an unbroken tradition of pilgrimage from the early Middle Ages until our own times. For devout pilgrims today the words of a fifteenth-century Welsh poet capture the mystical atmosphere of the place:

> And the breeze that comes from it
> Is as the honey-bees first swarming,
> A sweet odour over the turf
> Of musk or balm in the midst of the world . . .
>
> The drops of her blood are as the red shower
> Of the berries of the wild rose,
> The tears of Christ from the height of the Cross.

Cured Here
1794

Bardsey *The island of saints*

Bardsey Island lies off the tip of the Lleyn Peninsula in North Wales. Its name may originally have come from that of a Viking leader, but the Welsh call it Ynys Enlli, 'the Island of the Currents', on account of the swift tidal race between it and the mainland. After the departure of the Roman legions Bardsey became a refuge for Christian hermits. In the sixth century a Breton saint called Cadfan probably founded the earliest monastic community in Wales on the island. The fame of the holy island spread: to be buried on it became the desire of devout Christians in northern Wales, for they believed it to be the very porch of heaven. By the later Middle Ages men said that twenty thousand saints lay buried there, but this figure in medieval writings can usually be translated as 'a very great number'. Their graves occupied about four acres of the small island. An Augustinian abbey was established, dedicated to St Mary.

Pilgrims visited Bardsey throughout the Middle Ages. One of the great pilgrimage routes is marked by the churches of Clynnog Fawr (see p. 162), St Beuno's at Pistyll, Nevin, Llangwnnadl, and Aberdaron. Beyond Pistyll, on the left side of the road and just on a bend, you can see a small carved medieval cross within the stone walling. At Aberdaron the pilgrims embarked for Bardsey, and in the village stands a thirteenth-century building known as Y Gegin Fawr, 'the Big Kitchen', where they would be given a meal before setting out.

After the Reformation Bardsey was sold to a Caernarvonshire squire and became the haunt of fishermen and even pirates. Today, apart from a few farms and the huts of the bird sanctuary staff, it is a home of ruins and the bones of Celtic saints. Yet it is not difficult to imagine medieval pilgrims being ferried across crowded into the small wooden boats and perhaps nervously aware of the powerful tidal race.

Of the Celtic saints of Wales who may have visited the island or desired to be buried there, few memorials have survived, save for some small medieval chapels bearing their musical names on the sites of their original cells. At Pennant Melangell, near the village of Llangynog in a lovely Welsh valley, there stands a conjectural reconstruction of the shrine of St Melangell, in a small rectangular chapel known as Cell y Bedd, 'the Cell of the Grave'. To the south lies the church of Llanerfyl, which houses a simple fifteenth-century wooden reliquary carved in the shape of a church.

Left: *the 'Big Kitchen' at Aberdaron.*

Opposite: *Bardsey Island.*

Below: *a fifteenth-century wooden reliquary in Llanerfyl Church.*

Opposite: *the reconstructed shrine of St Melangell at Pennant Melangell, a rare example of a Romanesque shrine,* c. *1160–70.*

South Wales *St David and others*

During the sixth century monasteries sprang up across the Celtic fringe of Western Europe. David or Dewi, who became the patron saint of Wales, led the way in the southern half of that country, founding the first of his many monasteries on the site of the cathedral where his bones lie today. Pope Callixtus II in the early twelfth century stimulated pilgrims to the shrine by declaring that two pilgrimages to St David's equalled in merit one to Rome itself.

To this secluded corner of Wales came such royal pilgrims as William the Conqueror and Henry II, who paused on his way to Ireland to pray for victory and on his return journey to give thanks for it. In 1275 Bishop Richard de Carew constructed a new shrine for the relics, and the increased offerings of pilgrims at it enabled him to make progress with the rebuilding of the cathedral. This shrine can be seen today, occupying a bay on the north side of the presbytery. Above a stone seat for pilgrims there are openings through which they could reach with their hands and probably leave their offerings. Painted on the wall in the three arches above them, visible still in Elizabeth's reign, stood figures of St Patrick, St David and St Denis. The plain back of the shrine, projecting into the aisle, contains aumbries where relics or gifts were once displayed. A chest holding the chief relics would as usual have stood on the top. When not on display this chest may have been kept in a niche behind the high altar, where the bones of St David rest today in a modern reliquary.

Pilgrims would certainly have visited the chapel of St Non or Nona, the mother of David. Now a ruin, it lies near the shore half a mile south of the cathedral. To reach it you pass her well, which is kept in perfect order and guarded by a modern statue of the Saint. Opposite Ramsey Island, two miles west of St David's, stands the roofless chapel of St Justinian, a companion of David, which doubtless attracted some of the pilgrims to its door.

Three other shrines have survived in Welsh cathedrals. Beneath the same roof as St David's, in the north transept of the cathedral, there stands the restored thirteenth-century shrine of St Caradoc who asked to be buried there, a wish fulfilled in 1124. It is similar to that of St David; the step where pilgrims knelt can be seen, as well as the two quatrefoil holes where they placed their coins. At Llandaff Cathedral lay the bones of two sixth-century bishops, according to later legend the founder of the see and his successor – St Dubricius and St Teilo. Griffith, King of North Wales, witnessed the ceremony when the bones of Dubricius (who reputedly had crowned King Arthur) were carried into the cathedral, having been exhumed from their first resting place on Bardsey Island. When the monks washed the bones in three basins 'by the touch of the holy relics the water bubbled as if a red-hot stone had been thrown into it.' Dubricius lay on the north side of the presbytery and Teilo on the south. To swear 'upon the tomb of St Teilo and upon all the holy relics in the same church' was considered to be an especially solemn oath, and doubtless many contracts were sealed on it. In 1736 the cathedral architect opened St Teilo's coffin and saw the Bishop's sound corpse wrapped in leather, his pastoral staff, pewter cross and chalice at his side.

Other evidence of pilgrims remains on the road to St David's from Fishguard. Outside the door of St Brynach's Church at Nevern they would have seen a tall tenth-century cross, one of the most beautiful of the old Welsh crosses. Up the lane, where it forks to the right, you can find another cross carved by pilgrims on the rock, where doubtless they prayed for a safe journey. Yet not all pilgrims reached St David's or returned home to tell their tale. Six curious tombstones in the churchyard at Llanfihangel Abercywyn, a mile east of St Clears on the road between Carmarthen and St David's, may serve to remind us of this fact. In style they resemble the effigy of a pilgrim with hat, staff and scallop shell which rests beside the altar in the wayside church at Llandyfodwg, ten miles east of Cardigan. To the south lies Llandeilo Abercywyn, 'St Teilo's Church on the Mouth of the Cywyn', which possesses an old building (now used as a farmhouse) still called 'Pilgrims' Rest'.

In Pembrokeshire, wedged into the cliff on a precipitous headland, the tiny chapel of St Govan still evokes today the solitary life of the Celtic monk or hermit who once lived there. The site is ancient, dating back to the sixth century, although the present chapel was built some seven hundred years later. St Govan probably lies buried under the altar. On the left through an arched doorway is a niche where Govan hid from his pagan persecutors, the rock miraculously opening and closing behind him. Anyone who turns around in the niche is supposed to be assured of luck.

St David's Cathedral, seen from the gatehouse leading in to the abbey precincts. The east end is in the foreground.

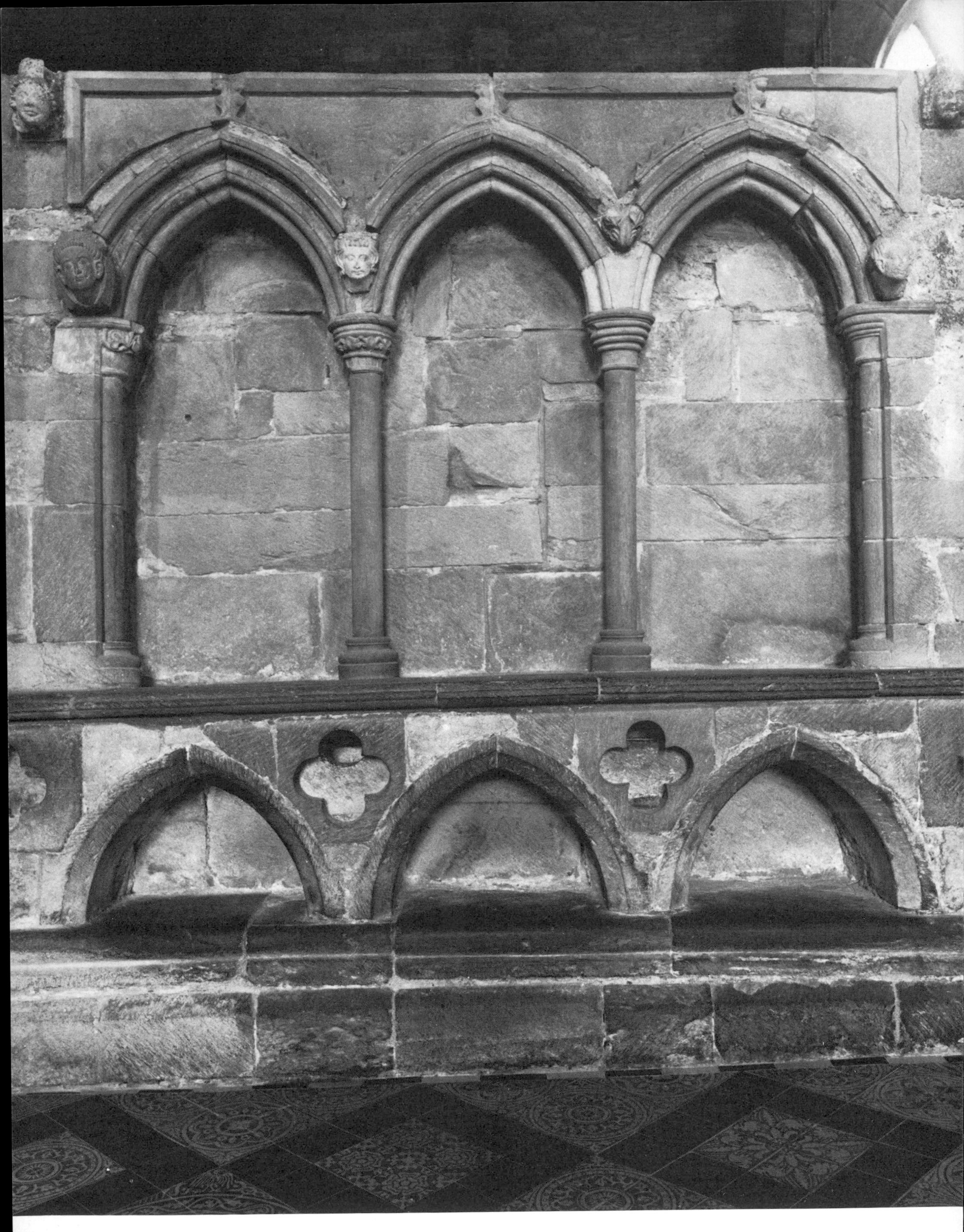

Opposite: *front of the shrine of St David.*

Right: *tomb of an unknown pilgrim in Llandyfodwg Church. In his right hand he holds a staff; he is wearing short boots, and over his shoulder hangs a tasselled scrip. The cockle shell on the left shows he had been to the shrine of St James of Compostela, and the crossed keys, symbolic of St Peter, suggest he had also been to Rome.*

Overleaf: *the tenth-century Cross of St Brynach, standing beside the church at Nevern that bears his name* (left), *and a wayside cross near Nevern carved by pilgrims going to St David's.*

Above: *medieval building, once part of a pilgrims' hospice, at Llandeilo Abercywyn.*

Below: *medieval tombstones near the castle at Llanfihangel Abercywyn.*

Opposite: *St Govan's Chapel.*

Scotland

Caledonia, a wild country of mountains and forests peopled by Celtic tribes, looked so formidable to the Romans that they abandoned their attempted conquest. The Scots, originally inhabitants of Ireland, crowned their earlier attempts at colonizing it by crossing over from Ulster to Argyll ('land of the Gael') about 500, and establishing a settlement. In the sixth century these Scots on the western coast heard the gospel from St Columba who came over to join them. (Not until the tenth century did the name Scotia cease to be applied to Ireland and become transferred to Scotland.)

The disciples and followers of Columba carried Christianity into the Western Highlands. The Macnabs, for example, claim descent from St Fillin, an eighth-century abbot. Tradition says that his left arm was luminous. The Macnabs laid any insane member of their clan on 'Fillin's Bed', a stone which marked his grave. In battle they fought behind his pastoral staff, which they believed to be a talisman.

The early inhabitants of Scotland were pagans, but there is no record of any violent conflict between them and the Celtic Christian missionaries. A Pictish queen did secure the death of St Donnan, who lived on the isle of Eigg near Iona, but he seems to have been the only martyr of the early Celtic Church in Scotland.

In the ninth century the King of the Scots also became King of the Picts, who inhabited eastern Scotland, thus uniting the Celtic peoples north of the firths of Forth and Clyde. These Pictish tribes had been visited by St Ninian and his followers. Later the Scottish kings tended to identify themselves with the Lowlands, which they gradually acquired. In the twelfth century King David I, third son of St Margaret, the Saxon royal heir who had fled at the Norman Conquest, and Malcolm Canmore (Macbeth's successor), pushed ahead with his mother's policy of imposing the Latin order on the Church, and by the end of his reign almost all the medieval sees had been founded. William the Conqueror invaded Scotland in 1072, initiating centuries of armed conflict and political tension between the two neighbouring realms.

The Reformation effected a complete revolution in the policy of Scotland and in the current of popular opinion. The sermons of John Knox and his fellow ministers won the hearts and minds of the common people in a way not achieved in England. Inspired by their iconoclastic pastors, the Scots made short work of destroying their medieval shrines. For the Reformers would not tolerate the old religion and such embedded practices as pilgrimage. The bones of St Margaret, enshrined at Dunfermline, ended up in a chapel built for them by King Philip II of Spain in the Escorial; her silver head reliquary found its way to the abbey of Douai in northern France.

The attempt of Charles I to impose the liturgy of the Church of England upon the Presbyterian Scots provoked them to their last major war against the English. After the Revolution of 1688 the English government at last acknowledged that it could not displace the Presbyterian Church system. Thus Scotland as a whole turned its back on the Catholic religion and all its works. Not until modern times, with a growth in the Catholic population, has interest re-awakened in the practice of pilgrimage.

Iona. In the foreground is the eleventh-century St Oran's Chapel, said to have been built by St Margaret on the site of St Columba's oratory. Part of the ancient cemetery of Reilig Odhrain can be seen around it, though the oldest tombstones have been removed to the site museum. Beyond is the abbey church, later a cathedral, built soon after 1200 and restored by the community who have resettled the abbey since 1938.

Iona *St Columba*

This famous Irish missionary and abbot who founded the monastery of Iona came originally from what is now County Donegal. 'In the forty-second year of his age,' wrote his biographer Adamnan, 'desiring to seek a foreign country for the sake of Christ, he sailed from Ireland to Britain.' With twelve companions Columba landed from his hide boat on the Scottish coast in about 563, and shortly afterwards resolved to build his monastery on Iona. This island, about three miles long and one or more in breadth, lies off the west coast of Scotland, separated from Mull by a narrow sound about half a mile wide.

From Iona Columba made long journeys through northern Scotland, preaching to the heathen Picts and setting up more monastic colonies. First he visited the Pictish pagans in Inverness, accompanied by St Kenneth and St Comgell who acted as interpreters. He also visited Carthures (Glasgow), where St Kentigern or Mungo ('the Beloved One') was at work among the tribes of Cumbria and Strathclyde. This saint, who had been trained in the school of St Serf in Fife, gave Columba a warm welcome, and they exchanged their pastoral staves on parting. It was Columba who gave the formal benediction to Aidan when he became King of the Scots (the earliest Christian coronation in British history) and in 575 accompanied him to Ireland, where he played a prominent part in the council held at Druim Ceata.

St Martin's Cross, with the cathedral behind it.

In retirement he probably gave some of his time to copying manuscripts, a monastic craft at which he excelled. The *Cathach* (a Psalter, in the Irish Academy Library at Dublin) is commonly ascribed to him, as well as three Latin hymns and some Gaelic poems. He frequently walked about the island, and on one occasion he sent a monk to rescue a storm-battered crane stranded on the rocks in Camus Bay. He spent many hours talking to the visitors who crossed over from Mull to see him, and at last died on the night of 8 June 597.

The body of Columba, known also as Colum (the Gaelic word for 'dove') or Columcille ('Colum of the Cell or Church'), attracted pilgrims to Iona within days of his death. There they saw his books and pastoral staff, the stone pillow on which he slept, and many other treasures. Writing in the late seventh century, Adamnan mentions the oaken church with a sacristy next to it, the refectory with a fireplace and stone water-trough where pilgrims washed their feet, the mill, barn and stable, and the individual beehive-shaped stone huts of the monks, with the Abbot's hut standing a little apart.

Norsemen raided Iona three times around 800, slaying sixty-eight monks at a place now known as Martyrs' Bay. In 825 the Danes landed again from their long ships and burst into the church, cutting down the Abbot and several monks as they celebrated Mass. Having ransacked the buildings they set fire to them and returned to their ships loaded with booty. The primacy of the Church in Scotland passed back to Kells in Ireland, and then to various other places before it became settled on the see of St Andrews. Meanwhile Iona slid into obscurity for all purposes except pilgrimage. In 980 Anlaf, King of the Danes around Dublin, came to live on the island after his defeat in battle, and died there as a penitent. Six years later, however, the Danes yet again ravaged the community, killing the Abbot and fifteen monks on the White Sands.

St Margaret rebuilt the destroyed abbey in 1072. In 1203 a Benedictine monastery was built nearby and soon afterwards a nunnery (later Augustinian) was founded on the island. For intermittent periods the Benedictine church, a cruciform building dedicated to St Mary, served as cathedral of a see which owed allegiance sometimes to the Archbishop of Trondjem in Norway and sometimes to the Primate of Scotland. After 1506, when it became the seat of the Bishop of the Isles, it was largely rebuilt in its present form. The cathedral was restored about 1900, and the Iona Community, founded in 1938, have rebuilt the abbey cloisters, sanctuary and sacristy and encouraged archaeological investigation, as well as adding new buildings.

No building stands on Iona today which has any association with St Columba, although archaeologists have established the outlines of the *vallum* (a ditch and earth bank) around his monastery and in 1957 their spades uncovered what may well have been the Abbot's cell. St Oran's Chapel, the oldest church on the island, is said to have been built by St Margaret on the site of St Columba's church. In the cathedral is a stone with an incised Celtic cross traditionally known as St Columba's Pillow, later his gravestone (for Adamnan relates that they set up the stone pillow as a monument at his grave). A small oratory to the north-west of the cathedral is believed to have once held the shrine of St Columba, but the relics had disappeared before the Benedictines arrived. Of the hundreds of crosses that once dotted the island several fragments remain, and two complete examples – the early St Martin's Cross (ninth- or tenth-century) which faces the cathedral door, and MacLean's Cross (probably fifteenth-century), farther away by the 'Street of the Dead', a track which runs inland from a landing place in Martyrs' Bay on the east shore of the island to Reilig Odhrain, the cemetery by St Oran's Chapel.

This ancient burial ground lies to the south-west of the cathedral. As in the case of Bardsey Island many Celtic Christians, both lay and clerical, eagerly sought the privilege of being buried here, perhaps inspired by the ancient prophecy:

> Seven years before the judgment,
> The sea shall sweep over Erin at one tide,
> And over blue-green Isla;
> But I of Colum of the Church shall swim.

Some sixty kings of Scotland, Ireland and Norway were buried in Reilig Odhrain, among them King Duncan. Shakespeare's lines in *Macbeth* echo the tradition:

> *Rosse* Where is Duncan's body?
> *Macduff* Carried to Columskill,
> The sacred storehouse of his predecessors,
> And guardian of their bones.

Beside them lay bishops, such as Hugh of the Crooked Legs, and a row of Maclean chieftains, including Ewan of the Little Head, who lost his life in a clan battle in the sixteenth century.

Many pilgrims would also visit the various cells or hermitages once occupied by holy men on the island and the Well of the North Wind, not far from one of them, where sailors and others brought offerings to conjure up a north wind. (The Well of the South Wind, which traditionally existed also, can no longer be found.) Superstition attends the one hill on the island: to make the ascent seven times, so pilgrims believed, brought them boundless good fortune. Its name, *Dun-I*, suggests that it may once have been crowned by a dry-stone fortress. Half-hidden behind a rocky outcrop on the northern brow of the hill lies a small pool known as the Well of the Age. Some who washed in it at dawn expected healing; others thought the waters would renew their lives, making them young in spirit again.

The Well of the Age.

On the Machair, the arable land in the middle west of the island, pilgrims who had read Adamnan would recall that the septuagenarian Columba had himself taken in a wheelchair here from the abbey to tell the monks toiling in the fields that his death was at hand. Not far away they could scramble up Angel's Hill, a grassy knoll better known by its old Gaelic name, Sithean Mor, 'the great fairy-mound'. Here the fairies of pre-Christian belief were thought to hold their revels. Adamnan relates that one day Columba ascended the hillock and stretched out his hands to heaven, whereupon a host of angels in white appeared about him. Thus pilgrims and native Islanders gathered there on the Feast of St Michael, hoping to see a vision of that Prince of Angels, Our Lady and Columba, whom they knew to be the guardians of Islemen sailing off the rocky coasts.

Perhaps one of the most evocative places on Iona is the Ridge of the Cliff, at the south-western corner of the island, where Columba is said to have stood after his first landing and looked out to sea to ensure that his Ireland, some seventy miles to the south, could not be seen lest its shadow on the horizon should tempt him back. Yet he came to love his new home, and may well have been the author of the prophesies which promised it survival throughout all the storms of history:

> In Iona of my heart, Iona of my love
> Instead of monks' voices shall be lowing of cows;
> But ere the world shall come to an end,
> Iona shall be as it was.

Opposite: *cross cut in the rock outside St Ninian's Cave.*
Above: *ruins of the church of Whithorn Priory.*

Overleaf: *St Ninian's Cave. Offerings of contemporary pilgrims – pebbles and a cross fashioned from driftwood – can be seen on the ledge.*

Whithorn *St Ninian*

Ninian, or Ninias, the first known apostle in Scotland, preached the gospel some time before St Columba arrived from Ireland. He built a church of white stone known as the White House (*Candida Casa*) at Whithorn in Galloway, and probably ministered from this base as a travelling bishop. Whether or not he studied in Rome and received his consecration as bishop there is a matter of scholarly dispute. Born on the shores of the Solway Firth, Ninian spent his life among his fellow countrymen until his death in 397. Their descendants kept his feast on 16 September.

Churches bearing Ninian's name have been traced all over the south and east of Scotland, stretching as far north as Caithness. Some believe that Ninian was the apostle to the southern Picts, just as Columba can be seen as the apostle to the Scots, but this view may be too simple. The ridge of mountains which forms the rocky spine of Scotland may have divided their two spheres of influence, but the evidence is far from conclusive.

Ninian was eventually buried in his 'White House', and for centuries his tomb attracted pilgrims of high and low estate. It is possible that a tomb beneath an arch of the presbytery in the remaining chancel of the ruined medieval priory church is his resting place. The kings and queens of Scotland head the list of distinguished pilgrims to his shrine, and in 1427 James I of Scotland offered his royal protection to all pilgrims going there wearing the prescribed badges. The names of those who thronged the roads of south-west Scotland have not survived, but there are several general references to the pilgrim traffic, such as a petition of a countess of Douglas to the Pope for an indulgence on the grounds that she had rebuilt a bridge over the River Bladnoch 'where pilgrims to St Ninian assemble'.

Pilgrims from Ireland and others travelling by sea landed at the safe harbour by the Isle of Whithorn, to the south-east. The ruins of a thirteenth-century church known as St Ninian's Kirk stand there on the site of an earlier chapel, which may have marked the place where St Ninian himself landed and from which his mission started. Four miles west, in a cliff face looking out over a pebbled beach across Port Castle Bay, there is a cave named after the Saint where he is said to have retired for prayer. Since the seventh or eighth century pilgrims have visited it, leaving some early crosses carved on the cave walls or on loose stones. Many can be seen in the museum at Whithorn. The pilgrims of today, who walk down the wooded valley to the sea and find the Saint's retreat marked by ancient crosses cut in the cliff, pick up large pebbles on the beach and scratch crosses on them so that they too can leave a sign of their devotion in the cave.

Orkney *St Magnus, a Viking saint*

The first Christians to land in Orkney and Shetland may have come from monasteries on the west coast of Scotland. Some traces of these early travellers, none earlier than the eighth century, survive on Shetland. On Barra, for example, archaeologists have uncovered the foundations of a settlement. In the stone panel of one tomb there are incised the figures of five monks in hooded capes, one on a horse and the others on foot, processing towards a cross. One carries a satchel containing relics or books. It may well commemorate the introduction of Christianity into the islands perhaps a century before.

The Norsemen conquered Orkney in the ninth century and it became a Scandinavian settlement. In the early eleventh century the inhabitants became Christians. Magnus, son of an earl of Orkney, showed his Christian spirit by refusing to wield his long axe in a sea-battle near Anglesey, declaring that he had no quarrel with the opposing crews. He sat on deck throughout the fighting reading a Psalter. For a time Magnus and his cousin ruled jointly as earls of Orkney, but the cousin had him slain on the small island of Egilsay. Within a short time of his death (in about 1117) the inhabitants of Orkney began to venerate him as St Magnus the Martyr.

A young man from Norway called Rognavald arrived in Orkney to claim a share in the earldom that had belonged to his uncle Magnus. After he had vowed to remove the Saint's relics to a new church his suit proved successful. Rognavald honoured his pledge, bringing skilled craftsmen from overseas for the purpose. The work of building the cathedral in red and yellow stone began in 1173, but three centuries passed before it had taken its present shape – probably just before the period of Norse rule in Orkney came to an end in 1468.

From the earliest days pilgrims came to the shrine of St Magnus, drawn by stories of the miraculous healing powers of his bones. Having worshipped at the shrine, they could buy a lead cross to sew on their hats or cloaks. A mould for making these crosses was found in the cathedral and can be seen there today.

At the time of the Reformation the remote situation of the cathedral preserved it from the worst excesses of the iconoclasts, and the clergy succeeded in hiding the relics. In 1919 they were discovered in a box behind a loose stone inside one of the oldest piers in the choir. The bones found in the opposite pier at the same time almost certainly belong to St Rognavald.

Medieval brass mould for making pilgrim crosses, shown with a lead cross cast in it.

Opposite: *looking east in St Magnus's Cathedral, Kirkwall. The heavy masonry of the arcade with its thick round columns is Norman; above that it becomes Gothic. The relics of St Magnus, and others thought to be of St Rognavald, are set into piers on either side of the high altar in the distance.*

Ireland

Pilgrimages in Ireland should be set against a backcloth of the civil and religious story of that tragic and yet lovely isle. The early history of its Celtic people is shrouded in a mist of obscurity which their most ancient myths do little to dispel. The Roman legions in the south and the German tribes to the north slowly drove the Celtic peoples of Europe out of their lands, so that when the light of recorded history shines on them with any clarity they held only the most western parts – namely, the Iberian Peninsula, Gaul and the British Isles.

Incessant tribal wars seem to have occupied the Celts in Ireland. Early in the second century a king of Meath established a nominal supremacy over the entire island, but Munster soon established its independence and further subdivisions followed. From the middle of the third century until the end of the fifth, Irish from both the northern and southern kingdoms planted their colonies in Britain. The former settled in North Wales, the Isle of Man and Scotland; the latter in South Wales, Devon and Cornwall. Meanwhile during the fifth century Christian missionaries from Gaul and Britain landed in Ireland and began the long work of converting the inhabitants. Among them came St Patrick, who possibly began his mission around the year 432.

In the early Celtic Church the tribe was sometimes reconstituted on a religious footing with the chief as the first abbot. A number of his tribesmen and women lived as celibates; many others practised fasting and prayer. The tribe chose the abbot's successors from his kin. For two centuries none but members of the same kin sat in the chair of St Patrick at Armagh, while the first eleven successors of Columba at Iona came from the same family as the Saint.

At an early date the monasteries became celebrated as centres of learning and craftsmanship. The monks excelled in illuminating manuscripts, producing such masterpieces as the *Book of Durrow* and, perhaps, the *Book of Kells*. They also finely worked metals, precious stones and leather. The sixth-century monastery of St Kevin at Glendalough achieved great fame for scholarship. Its many early remains include 'St Kevin's Kitchen', a primitive stone-roofed chamber. The early stone beehive cells on the towering rock called Skellig Michael, off the Kerry coast, also help to give us some idea of what an Irish monastery looked like. Tall round towers, such as those at Glendalough and Clonmacnoise, served these religious communities as belfries, places of refuge and lookout points: about a hundred remain in various states of repair. The primitive churches in such settlements are best exemplified today by the Gallarus Oratory on the Dingle Peninsula in Kerry. In outline it resembles an inverted boat. Made entirely of stones without any mortar, it has kept the rain out for fifteen centuries.

Opposite: *the mountain of Croagh Patrick, scene of the main pilgrimage to St Patrick, one of Ireland's 'Three Patrons' (see p. 195).* Below: *the Gallarus Oratory.*

In 795 the Vikings in their long ships reached the Irish coast and carried away their first cargoes of booty and slaves. In later years they returned in ever larger numbers, endeavouring to conquer the islands and settle there. In a battle on Good Friday in 1014, however, the Christian Irish tribes decisively defeated the Norse followers of Thor and Odin, thereby ensuring that Ireland would remain under the cross.

The Christian Normans in the twelfth century proved to be more successful conquerors, and they sought to impose the Latin forms of Christianity in the lands controlled by them. The Pope sent St Malachy to Ireland to introduce the new disciplines. He found the Church there in a parlous condition. The Norse invaders had sacked many of the monasteries, while lay patrons had secured control of their lands. The hereditary Archbishop of Armagh vacated his seat in favour of Malachy, and the other Irish bishops came to acknowledge him as Primate of Ireland. Shortly afterwards he decided to return to Rome, doubtless to report progress. At Clairvaux Abbey he left his companions with St Bernard (founder of the Cistercian order) for instruction and journeyed on alone. Pope Innocent II acknowledged his achievement by appointing him papal legate in Ireland. On his return Malachy founded the Cistercian monastery of Mellifont in County Louth, the first in Ireland to adopt that rule. Eight years later he died at Clairvaux, far from Ireland but near to the heart of the monastic tradition which he so clearly loved. Another Cistercian house founded in this period, Holycross Abbey in County Tipperary, once contained a relic of the True Cross. It is believed by some that a remarkable openwork structure between two chapels in the south transept may have been designed for the exhibition of the relic. The Gothic church, long a ruin, was recently re-roofed and restored, and it has acquired another relic of the Cross, set in a precious portable reliquary.

The shrine of Our Lady of Knock. The vision of Our Lady, St Joseph and St John the Evangelist appeared outside the church on the left. The spot is now marked by an altar with their statues, protected by the glass structure. In the background some of the Stations of the Cross can be seen, before the new pilgrims' church.

The abbey of Holycross, seen across the River Drish. From right to left, the abbey church (its chancel lit by the large traceried window), ruins of the pilgrim's hospice, and the abbey waterwheel.

The Norman conquest and settlement of Ireland allowed the king of England to claim the feudal allegiance of the Irish kings, but the connection remained loose until the sixteenth century when Henry VIII and Elizabeth, fearing an alliance between Catholic Ireland and England's enemies, determined to secure the country by sending over numerous Protestant 'colonists', who settled most thickly in Ulster. The Irish and those few Anglo-Irish who were Catholics rose together against their English overlords in 1641, only to be crushed by Oliver Cromwell. The defeat of James II in 1691 removed the faint hope that Ireland could establish itself as an independent Catholic kingdom. A relic of these religious upheavals, the mummified head of St Oliver Plunkett, Archbishop of Armagh, who was martyred on the scaffold at Tyburn in 1681 (and canonized in 1975), rests grimly in a glass-fronted reliquary in St Peter's Church in West Street, Drogheda. His body is enshrined in the Benedictine abbey of Downside in England. Not until this century did southern Ireland become a separate state, under the name of Eire.

The fact that the Irish remained predominantly Catholic throughout the centuries means that pilgrimage has continued as an integral and living religious practice down to the present day. For example, about 750,000 pilgrims a year visit the shrine of Our Lady of Knock, at the parish church in County Mayo where a number of people saw an apparition of the Blessed Virgin which lasted two hours on the evening of 21 August 1879. Our Lady's Island, some five miles south of Rosslare in County Wexford, is another place of Marian pilgrimage. For centuries pilgrims have traversed the causeway which joins it to the mainland, chiefly on 15 August, the Feast of the Assumption. There is a shrine to the Virgin, and the ruins of the Augustinian abbey of St Mary.

HOLYCROSS

Left: *carving of the Virgin and Crucified Christ above which the relic of the True Cross is now displayed, on the north side of the sanctuary.*

Below left: *a silver portable reliquary containing a large fragment of the True Cross. It is known to have belonged in 1633 to Walter Butler, the last Catholic Earl of Ormonde, and the Butler family recently presented it to Holycross Abbey Church. Constant touching has worn the wood beneath the little quatrefoil window, which could be opened for that purpose.*

Opposite: *the table tomb or shrine in the south transept of the church.*

Downpatrick, Croagh Patrick and Lough Derg *St Patrick*

Son of Calpurnius, a Roman *decurio* (a minor local official) and later a Christian deacon, Patrick was born in Britain. Irish raiders captured him at the age of sixteen, and transported him into slavery. For six years he shepherded his owner's flocks 'in the woods and on the mountain . . . in snow, frost and rain'. Then he escaped to the coast, and joined a ship bound for the Continent with a cargo of hounds. After a stormy voyage of three days the ship made landfall on a barren coast. The company wandered through a wilderness for a month before they reached civilization. Eventually Patrick made his way to England. But in thoughts and dreams he heard persistently 'the voice of the Irish' calling him back. He returned as a bishop to Ireland, where he endured many hardships and at least one sojourn in prison. Despite all he carried the Christian faith into regions untouched by other missionaries and made many converts. This sparse outline of Patrick's life can be constructed from two short works he wrote himself, the *Confessio* and *Epistola ad milites Corotici* (a letter addressed to the British chieftain Coroticus), supplemented by early medieval biographies.

Patrick is said to have died at the abbey of Saul (or Sabbhall) on 17 March 461, but neither place nor date is certain. His relics were laid to rest in the abbey of Downpatrick, where they were later joined by the reputed bones of St Bridget and St Columba, the two other tutelary saints of Ireland. Subsequently the Danes burnt the town and pillaged the cathedral six or seven times. In the twelfth century an Anglo-Norman baron seized the town and held it by force. Thirteen years later he replaced the canons with a community of Benedictine monks drawn from the abbey of St Werburgh at Chester. By this time no one knew the location of the relics of Ireland's 'Three Patrons', but in 1185 Malachy III, Bishop of Down, claimed to have seen in a vision a tomb with these words inscribed in Latin upon it:

> In Down, three saints one grave do fill:
> Patrick, Brigid and Columcille.

When the Bishop found the coffin thus marked great joy prevailed throughout Ulster. In the following year the papal legate transferred the relics into more splendid shrines. Possibly they lie now under a huge boulder marked 'Padraic' in a small graveyard adjoining the modern Church of Ireland cathedral at Downpatrick. At various times Saul, Downpatrick, Durham, Dunkeld and Glastonbury have all claimed that they alone possessed the bones of St Patrick.

One of Ireland's great historic sites, the Rock of Cashel in County Tipperary, has very early associations with St Patrick. It was the seat of the kings of Munster from about the fourth century until the twelfth, when it passed into the hands of the Church. The fine ruins which crown the rock include the arcaded Norman front of Cormac's Chapel.

Today the main pilgrimage associated with St Patrick is on the mountain of Croagh Patrick in County Mayo, which lifts itself suddenly from the lowland on the southern shore of Clew Bay into a conical summit of white rock. Here the Saint is said to have lived during the forty days of Lent in 441, in a hut on a site now marked by a heap of stones, fighting manfully against the temptations of demons. A major pilgrimage by up to eighty thousand people takes place on the last Sunday in July, the so-called Garland or Garlic Sunday. A Mayo legend relates that a witch threw garlic water at Patrick to kill him as part of a spell: the Saint promptly hurled back a hand-bell (which Celtic missionaries carried) and it slew her on the spot. After angels had succoured him, Patrick is reputed to have prayed on this mountain that Ireland might never lose the faith he had preached to it.

Opposite: *the reputed burial place of St Patrick, St Bridget and St Columba at Downpatrick.* Below: *A 'penal' crucifix from St Patrick's Purgatory, dated 1785. (National Museum of Antiquities of Scotland, Edinburgh).*

Some of the many thousands of pilgrims still climb the mountain barefooted. The first station is a mound of rock and stone at the foot of the final rise to the summit, called after St Brendan. Here the pilgrim says seven Paters, seven Aves and one Credo, while making seven circuits of the mound. The practice of walking round holy places or wells in a clockwise direction, universal in Ireland, may go back to the days of sun-worship, when the pagan worshipper walked around a stone or circle in the direction of the sun. At the second station, the modern chapel and 'Patrick's Bed', as the cell site is called, the pilgrim repeats this observance. The third and final station lies on a continuation of the ridge of Croagh Patrick to the west about half a mile away, a place dedicated to the Virgin Mary. At one time a custodian family used to produce for a small fee on pilgrimage days St Patrick's Bell, and each pilgrim kissed the shape of a cross upon it and passed it three times around his body. Many pilgrims completed their days with a visit to Kilgeever well and its ancient ruined church near Croagh Patrick.

The Irish made pilgrimages not only to the lonely mountain eyries of their saints but also to the islands where they often withdrew for prayer or habitation. A good example of these island pilgrimages is Lough Derg in Donegal. The name of one St Mobeoc or Dabeoc is associated with the lake; he may have presided over a Celtic monastery on Saint's Island. But he was not the author of the island's fame. In the twelfth century a knight called Owen spent a fortnight in prayer and fasting beside Lough Derg, culminating in a vigil lasting a day and night in a cave on Station Island in the Lough. He saw himself in visions being led through heaven and hell, and these adventures he related to Gilbert of Louth, a monk from Lincolnshire. Gilbert told the tale to a Cistercian monk who wrote an account of this miraculous Irish island. In it the monk told of a tradition that St Patrick, being unable to convince his audience of the reality of hell and purgatory, prayed to God for some visual aid. In answer he was shown the cave on Station Island, a place where the doubters could experience the next world if they dared. Hence the island became known as St Patrick's Purgatory.

The island achieved some fame in Europe in the Middle Ages and pilgrims flocked there. The Church controlled it closely, and the pilgrim had to obtain expensive passports for his venture into purgatory from the diocesan bishop and the prior of the Augustinian house which had custody of the island. Some pilgrims, it was rumoured, never returned from the cave; many others, however, emerged into the daylight somewhat disgruntled that they had not seen or experienced the terrors of the afterlife. One such disappointed pilgrim, a Dutchman, complained to Rome that the cave was a fraud. In 1497 the Pope ordered it to be closed 'as it was not the one pointed out to St Patrick'. But the pilgrims still came, and in 1503 the Archbishop of Armagh successfully petitioned the Pope to revoke the order and to grant indulgences to those who came. Later attempts to stamp out the pilgrimage proved quite futile. The local people carved wooden crosses for the pilgrims to take away as tokens, and some early primitive ones have survived, as well as more numerous later examples.

Today the pilgrimage to Lough Derg is essentially a penitential one. During his three days there the pilgrim eats and drinks frugally. He arrives on the island fasting on the first day, takes off his shoes and goes barefooted for the rest of the time. During the long series of devotions at the various Stations he visits St Patrick's Cross, St Bridget's Cross and the ruins of six beehive cells or 'beds', which are named by convention after saints. Prayers are recited here as the pilgrim walks around the cells. At the water's edge, where more prayers are said, the ancestors of today's pilgrims plunged into the cold waters of the lake, a custom based on the practice by Celtic monks of mortifying the flesh by standing immersed in lake or river while praying or singing Psalms. The whereabouts of the cave pointed out to St Patrick can no longer be identified on the small island which is now crowded with modern buildings.

Façade of King Cormac's Chapel on the Rock of Cashel.

Fauchart *St Bridget*

St Bridget's Well. Rags are hung as close as possible to the spring.

Opposite: *two of the many shrines at Fauchart. Near the Calvary Shrine* (above) *the bushes are hung with pieces of cloth.*

Bridget, *alias* Brigid, Brigida and Bride, came to prominence as Abbess of Kildare in the sixth century. Apart from legend, myth and folklore, little is known about her life. These most dubious authorities tell us that she was born at Fauchart, now in County Louth, of a noble father and slave mother. A Druid bought her mother and herself but Bridget later converted him to Christianity. When she was reunited with her father, he resolved to marry her to the King of Ulster. Seeing her piety and steadfast adherence to virginity, however, her royal bridegroom bowed to the inevitable and helped her to found a nunnery at Kildare.

Bridget is said to have died on 1 February somewhere about the year 526. Stories about her are much confused by pagan motifs, and it is hard to extricate fact from fiction. Indeed 1 February is also Imbolg, the pagan Irish festival of spring. Again there is a pleasing association between this Celtic saint and the birds: the Gaelic name for the oyster-catcher is *gille-brigde*, 'the servant of Bride'.

In time the abbey grew in size and by the early eighth century it had become a double house, for both monks and nuns. A partition down the middle divided their common church; the richly decorated shrines of Bridget and Bishop Conlaed, one of the earliest abbots, stood on the right and left of the single altar behind a screen dividing the nave from the chancel. Gold and silver crowns hung over the two shrines.

Today Bridget is honoured as a patron saint of Ireland, and her reputed birthplace at Fauchart is the goal of many Irish pilgrims. The present shrine, built in 1933, contains a portion of her head. South-west of the ruined old church runs St Bridget's Stream, near whose source pilgrims hang pieces of cloth on the trees. Some scholars believe that this ancient practice, which is widespread in Ireland and occurs in Scotland as well, is an echo of primitive tree worship; others think that the rags originally came from the clothes of sick people and were brought by their relatives to hang near the water, perhaps as votive offerings. The pilgrims visit various sites, marked by shrines and statues, associated with the Saint, such as a rock which shows the impression of her knee where she knelt.

Celtic Irish pilgrimages

No records of Irish pilgrims in the early Middle Ages have survived, but we can form a composite picture of the object of their pilgrimages. Usually they walked to a religious community in their tribal territory where some holy monk had lived and died, possibly one who had preached the gospel in their houses and healed their children. He would be accorded the title of 'saint' in keeping with the universal practice of those days. Before the Roman Church introduced some order into the proceedings, the people made a saint by word of mouth: sanctity of life and the association of miracles with the living person or his body usually sufficed to have him so named. Apart from some legends, little or nothing is commonly known about these Celtic saints.

In some instances the saint had lived alone, and the pilgrims merely visited his cell and the spring where he drew water. They walked around them a specified number of times clockwise in the direction of the sun, saying short prayers known by heart, such as the Lord's Prayer. The custom of repeating many times a phrase, sentence or short prayer has been traced back by some historians to the Desert Fathers, who took refuge in the wilderness of Egypt in the early Christian centuries. It is a practice well suited to illiterate people and also more convenient than reading from books for those walking over stony ground, as many pilgrims do.

Where the saint lived in community or where a monastery had grown up around his tomb, the pilgrim found himself in a small religious settlement. The erstwhile home of a sixth-century saint called St Ciaran at Clonmacnoise, on the banks of the River Shannon in County Offaly, serves as a good example of such a community, especially as it is still the resort of pilgrims today. A round tower, oratory and holy wells stand near the cathedral. The Celtic Cross of Clonmacnoise is perhaps the finest of its kind in Ireland. The relics of the Saint are no more, but his crozier can be seen.

Two outstanding examples of the reliquaries which once held the bones of Celtic saints have survived. The *Breac Maodhóg*, or shrine of St Moedoc, once contained the relics of the sixth-century founder of the monastery of Ferns. For many years it was kept in the church of St Moedoc at Drumlane, where the priest sometimes lent it for swearing upon at trials, but it is now in the National Museum of Ireland. In the usual form for such a reliquary, the *Breac Maodhóg* is a rectangular casket with a steep roof, about 9 inches long, 7¼ inches high and 3½ inches thick. These dimensions suggest that it may once have been called the *Bracc Maodhóg*, or 'hand of Moedoc', and have served as a hand reliquary. It is made of pale bronze, covered with gilt plates of figures in relief. Associated with it is the *Cumdach*, a leather satchel and strap with

The reliquary of St Moedoc, or Breac Maodhóg. *Rings in the ends allowed it to be carried on a strap. (National Museum of Ireland, Dublin)*

Opposite: *Clonmacnoise. MacCarthy's Church, of the twelfth century, and its associated round tower are seen through a window of the cathedral. This round tower, like the one at Cashel, is unusual in that it can be entered from inside the church as well as outside.*

which the shrine was carried through the provinces of the clan. One early account relates that the boy Benen with a satchel on his back followed St Patrick, while it is recorded that St Fiacc received as a present such a *cumdach* with among other things a reliquary in it.

St Manchan, an even more shadowy seventh-century saint (*manach* may come from the Latin *monachus*, meaning monk), was possibly Abbot of Leith. According to a twelfth-century chronicler the last high-king covered 'the shrine of Manchan or Maethail . . . and an embroidering of gold was carried over it by him in as good a style as a relic was ever covered in Ireland'. This description accords well with the reliquary now preserved on the altar of a chapel in Boher, in the parish of Lemanaghan in Offaly, which lies near the ruined Leith Abbey. Some think that this remarkable object was made at the monastery of Clonmacnoise, or that it was an earlier wooden shrine adorned with decorated metalwork by the monks of Clonmacnoise.

St Manchan's Reliquary is made of yew wood plated with bronze, gilt and enamel. Only ten figures out of about fifty-two remain grouped under the large cross: they wear close-fitting tunics with an outer sleeved garment, and below their girdles richly embroidered philibegs or kilts. Their legs and feet are bare. One carries an axe, another a book and two others short swords, while one has a steel helmet on his head. They wear their hair and beards trimmed in different ways. It is difficult to resist the conclusion that whatever the identity of these subjects (possibly Biblical), the twelfth-century craftsman took as his models the Irish clansmen who came as pilgrims to seek the blessing of St Manchan. The chest still contains some bones and the greater part of a human skull.

Besides pilgrims to such shrines of the saints, either within Ireland or beyond its shores, there were *peregrini* who travelled with no fixed destination in mind. The *Anglo-Saxon Chronicle* records that in 891 'three Scots [that is, Irish] came to King Alfred in a boat without oars from Ireland, whence they had stolen away, because they desired for the love of God to be in a state of pilgrimage, they cared not whither.' Had not St Columbanus spoken of life as a roadway, where Christians must travel in perpetual pilgrimage, as guests of the world? But this trusting of oneself to the Lord of the Elements became less possible as on the one hand the Church came to favour stability among its monks and, on the other, the Vikings infested the seas. The true heirs of these pilgrims, who sought only solitude and salvation, were the anchorites. 'All alone in my little cell,' wrote one ninth-century poet, 'such a pilgrimage would be dear to my heart. Even so, the early *peregrini* who blew like dandelion seeds along the western seaways led to Christianity taking root upon many a rocky headland or sea-girt cove in the British Isles.

A figure playing the Irish harp, on one end of the Breac Maodhóg. *(National Museum of Ireland, Dublin)*

The pilgrimage of everyman

We have come to the end of this journey made in the footsteps of the medieval pilgrims in Britain and Ireland. There have been many rewards: interesting people and unusual sights, stories and glimpses into history. But what does it all mean for us today?

Recent historians have tended to over-emphasize the medical and penitential aspects of pilgrimage. The sick and barefooted formed only a tiny minority of the multitudes who came to the shrines. The others, I have surmised, were seeking a bridge between the present and the past. As I have said, most of them would have possessed concrete, literal minds in an age dominated by theological abstractions and generalities. They were people, like the disciple Thomas, who longed to *see* and *touch* their Lord and his world. Relics were visible and tangible. Moreover, to the faithful, their particles remained charged with that mysterious force which some men called 'holy', and which we still do not fully understand. 'Lord, I believe, help thou my unbelief.'

We are also caught in the same dilemma. God is abstract; we are concrete. We look for materials which can serve as a bridge or means of approach. For us, the appropriate 'relics' may be fossils in the ground, protons in a high energy accelerator, or even a piece of moon rock. Thus science is a major part of the unfolding meaning of pilgrimage today. St Thomas (Becket)'s Hospital in London replaces St Thomas Becket's Shrine at Canterbury. Indeed nature itself becomes one vast relic of a forgotten Creator.

Within the narrower compass of religion, the last century of Biblical scholarship and archaeology can be understood as the continuation of pilgrimage by other means. For at its heart is the quest for the historical Jesus. Apart from the fact that Jesus and his early followers remain elusive to the historian, this devoted study of literary relics and artefacts has a major drawback: like science it is the preserve of scholars, not the common ground of the people.

Behind pilgrimage lies the idea of a journey. Possibly the desire to travel reflects some deeper memory in our unconscious mind of the migrational journeys of our distant ancestors. Certainly it surfaces with varying intensity. You or I may take a package tour or go on a walking holiday, while fellow men more intrepid undertake their journeys of a lifetime, crossing the snowy icefields of Antarctica or the sands of the Sahara. Some might say that man the traveller has merely doffed the religious clothes of a pilgrim, which he wore in those brief Christian centuries poised between saga voyage and scientific expedition. But pilgrimages in the wider sense are journeys with spiritual meaning. The great journeys of all ages (and in our own lives) have been those with some meaning for the soul of the traveller. Therefore, it could be argued, we need journeys for our spiritual life today, and those who undertake great ones do so as our representatives, providing – and it is a big 'if' – they can share with us their deeper experiences.

There remains to be discussed that sublime analogy between such definite journeys and an individual's journey through life. Even before the times when St Paul could tell his converts that they were 'strangers and pilgrims' on the face of the earth, doubtless preachers had used the journey image to illuminate the spiritual significance of life. Behind Bunyan's *Pilgrim's Progress* there lay a number of medieval allegories, not least the *Vision of Piers Ploughman* (which has been quoted earlier). But Bunyan the tinker, one of the lower artisan class which once much frequented the saints' shrines, put flesh and blood on allegory. Paradoxically, his work was most successful because he had such a concrete mind as well as a profound first-hand knowledge of what he was writing about.

Yet Bunyan's characters in their seventeenth-century clothes are as remote from us as Chaucer's pilgrims. We can neither go to Becket's tomb nor take the life journey prescribed for us by Puritan theology. But just as we can respond to the humanity of Chaucer's pilgrims so we can recognize ourselves in Bunyan's figures of Christian and Christiana. The Slough of Despond, the Hill of Difficulty and even the dungeons of Giant Despair are places on the maps of modern life. Moreover, we are dimly aware that those we encounter on the road – still more our companions over short or long stretches of it – are, for good or ill, both changing us and being changed in an unspoken conversation of human spirits. We may be less certain than previous ages about our destination – what awaits us at the end of our pilgrimage beyond the allegorical river of death. At least we are coming to believe again that we are set upon a journey with a spiritual meaning, and that hope, faith and love make tolerable travelling companions.

Those who hold with me a contemporary version of the view that life is a pilgrimage must constantly return to the experience of physical journeys if the image is to remain spiritually sustaining. The present is so fleeting, and our own lives so limited, that we have to feed upon other people's travels in history. Medieval pilgrimages in the British Isles belong within this context, those countless faint lines of human footsteps that traverse the globe in significant journeys from time immemorial. With our limited knowledge of what is possible, living in a world yet more wonderful than we can imagine, we should be wise to refrain from looking down upon the beliefs and practices of those pilgrims who travelled to the saints' shrines. For we are spiritual wayfarers also, and we may well reflect upon the old English proverb: 'God knows well who are the best pilgrims'.

Acknowledgments

For their kindness and courtesy in allowing me to photograph the subjects in this book, I am indebted to the following:

Rev. J. E. Bowers, St Helen's, Ashby-de-la-Zouch; Father Brennen, The Friary, Aylesford; Rev. Harrison, Beverley Minster; Canon Lawler, The Administrator, St Chad's Cathedral, Birmingham; Rev. Barrie, St Petroc's, Bodmin; The Rev. Father, Boher; Bramley Parochial Church Council; The Dean and Chapter of Canterbury Cathedral; Debenhams Ltd, Canterbury; Rev. R. J. C. Lloyd, St Mary the Virgin, Chartham; The Dean and Chapter of Chester Cathedral; The Vicar, St Beuno, Clynnog Fawr; Rev. R. A. W. Hambly, St Nicholas, Compton; Derby Museums and Art Gallery; Custodian of the Shrine, St Peter's, Drogheda; The Dean and Chapter of Durham Cathedral; National Museum of Antiquities of Scotland, Edinburgh; The Dean and Chapter of Ely Cathedral; Rev. B. Peters, St Etheldreda, Ely; Mr L. G. Ashby, Custodian, Glastonbury Abbey; The Glastonbury Antiquarian Society; Somerset Rural Life Museum, Glastonbury; The Dean and Chapter of Gloucester Cathedral; Dr G. Brade-Birks, Godmersham; The Trustees of St Nicholas Hospital, Harbledown; The Dean and Chapter of Hereford Cathedral; Bishop Anthony Hunter, Hexham Abbey; Father Lynch, Holycross Abbey; Canon Matthew J. Kelly, St Winifride's, Holywell; Rev. Roger Balkwell, Ilam; Iona Community; Rev. T. H. J. Hawkins, St Cedd, Lastingham; The Dean and Chapter of Lichfield Cathedral; The Dean and Chapter of Lincoln Cathedral; The Vicar, Glynogwr, Llandyfodwg; Rev. Ceri Evans, Llanerfyl; Museum of London; Rev. P. A. Lawrence, North Marston; The Dean and Chapter of Norwich Cathedral; Orkney Island Council; The Dean and Chapter of Christ Church, Oxford, The Vicar, Pennant Melangell; Rev. R. I. N. Edwards, St John the Baptist, Plymtree; Rev. F. J. H. Lisemore, St Wystan, Repton; The Very Rev. P. C. Moore, The Dean, Cathedral and Abbey Church of St Alban; The Very Rev. Lawrence Bowen, The Dean, St Davids Cathedral; The Hon. John St Aubyn, St Michael's Mount; Rev. R. B. Sawle, St Neot; Rev. Philip Seal, St James's, Shere; Rev. J. R. C. Lumley, Abbey Church, Shrewsbury; Rev. Peter Hollis, St Gregory's, Sudbury; Gainsborough's House Society, Sudbury; Rev. A. V. Carefull, The Administrator, The Shrine of Our Lady of Walsingham; The Walsingham Estate Office; The Dean and Chapter of Westminster Abbey; Rev. Robert Raikes, Whitchurch Canonicorum; The Dean and Chapter of Winchester Cathedral; Canon K. W. H. Felstead, Master of St Cross, Winchester; The Dean and Chapter of Worcester Cathedral; The Dean and Chapter of York; Mr M. S. Marks; The National Trust; Department of the Environment, England; The Scottish Office; The Welsh Office; Commissioner of Public Works, Ireland.

In particular, I would like to acknowledge the help given to me by clergy, vergers, beadles, curators, librarians, keepers, maintenance staff and all professional and voluntary workers upon whose dedicated care the churches, museums and historic heritage of Great Britain and Ireland depend.

P.C.-B.

In addition, the publishers would like to thank the following for supplying photographs or allowing them to be reproduced: Cambridge University Library 76; National Museum of Ireland, Dublin 200, 202; The Board of Trinity College, Dublin 124; The Dean and Chapter of Durham Cathedral 146; The Librarian, Glasgow University Library 45 *below left*; British Library, London 8, 36, 45 *top*, 66, 104, 107, 112, 113 *below*, 120, 125 *below*; courtesy the Trustees of the British Museum, London 74, 75; courtesy Messrs Craddock and Barnard, London 163 *below*; Lambeth Palace Library, London 117 *below*; Museum of London 12, 13, 118; National Monuments Record 57; Society of Antiquaries, London 102; University College, Oxford 143, 145; Henry E. Huntingdon Library and Art Gallery, San Marino Calif. 45 *below right*; Lichtbildwerkstätte 'Alpenland', Vienna 4.

Maps drawn by David Eccles.

Select bibliography

Unless otherwise stated, the place of publication is London

GENERAL

R. M. Clay, *The Medieval Hospitals of England* (1966); D. J. Hall, *English Medieval Pilgrimage* (1965); S. Heath, *In the Steps of the Pilgrims* (1950); C. Hole, *English Shrines and Sanctuaries* (1954); R. C. Hope, *The Legendary Lore of the Holy Wells of England* (1893); G. H. Jones, *Celtic Britain and the Pilgrim Movement* (1912); J. J. Jusserand, *English Wayfaring life in the Middle Ages* (2nd ed. 1920); C. G. Loomis, *White Magic: An Introduction to the Folklore of Christian Legend* (Cambridge, Mass., 1948); H. F. M. Prescott, *Jerusalem Journey* (1954); C. Thomas, *Britain and Ireland in Early Christian Times AD 400–800* (1971); K. Thomas, *Religion and the Decline of Magic* (1971); J. C. Wall, *The Shrines of British Saints* (1905); C. K. Zacher, *Curiosity and Pilgrimage: the literature of discovery in fourteenth-century England* (Baltimore, Md, 1976)

ON SAINTS

A. E. Abbot, *St Thomas of Canterbury: His Death and Miracles* (1898); D. Attwater, ed., *The Penguin Dictionary of Saints* (Harmondsworth, Mx, 1965); C. F. Battiscombe, ed., *The Relics of St Cuthbert* (Oxford, 1956); W. de G. Birth, *Memorials of St Guthlac of Crowland* (Wisbech, Cambs., 1881); A. Jessopp and M. R. James, *Thomas of Monmouth's Life and Miracles of St William of Norwich* (Cambridge, 1896); D. Knowles, *Saints and Scholars* (Cambridge, 1962); R. Knox and S. Leslie, *The Miracles of King Henry VI* (Cambridge, 1923). See also Fowler, below.

ON PLACES

J. C. Dickinson, *The Shrine of Our Lady of Walsingham* (Cambridge, 1956); Erasmus, *Ten Colloquies*, transl. and ed. C. R. Thompson (New York, 1957), and *Pilgrimages to St Mary of Walsingham and St Thomas of Canterbury*, transl. and ed. J. G. Nichols (1875); J. Fowler, 'On a window representing the life and miracles of St William of York', *Yorkshire Archaeological and Topographical Journal*, III (York, 1875), pp. 198–348; S. Jennett, *The Pilgrim's Way from Winchester to Canterbury* (1971); F. M. McNeill, *Iona: A History of the Island* (Edinburgh, 1920); N. Pevsner, ed., *The Building of England* series (Harmondsworth, Mx, 1951ff.); A. P. Stanley, *Historical Memorials of Canterbury* (11th ed. 1887); R. F. Treharne, *Glastonbury Legends* (1967); C. Wilson, *The Shrines of St William of York* (Yorkshire Museum, York, 1977).

Index

Numbers in *italic* type refer to illustrations. For convenience, both old and new county names are given where applicable, the new in brackets.